Bicycling Magazine's

Nutrition
for
Cyclists

By the Editors of *Bicycling* Magazine

Rodale Press, Emmaus, Pennsylvania

Bicycling Magazine is a registered trademark of Rodale Press, Inc.

Printed in the United States of America on acid-free ∞ , recycled paper ♻

Compiled by *Ed Pavelka*

Edited by *Kathleen Becker*

Production editor: *Jane Sherman*

Copy editor: *Durrae Johanek*

Cover and interior design: *Lisa Farkas*

Cover photo: *Ed Landrock*

Library of Congress Cataloging-in-Publication Data

Bicycling magazine's nutrition for cyclists/by the editors of Bicycling magazine.
     p.   cm.
   ISBN 0–87857–935–4 paperback
   1. Cyclists—Nutrition.   I. Bicycling!   II. Title: Nutrition for cyclists.
TX361.C94B53   1991
613.2′0247966—dc20   90–25277
                                                                CIP

Distributed in the book trade by St. Martin's Press

    6   8   10   9   7   paperback

CONTENTS

 **INTRODUCTION**

One of the best things about being a bike rider occurs when you sit at the dinner table, because the best foods for cycling also happen to be the most fun to eat. Even better, as this book will explain, they are the best foods for sound, lifelong nutrition and good health.

We're speaking of carbohydrate-rich foods, which supply energy while avoiding most dietary dangers, such as fat and cholesterol. Fruits, vegetables, grains, breads, pasta—you'll read about these and other excellent choices in the following pages. There are also chapters on foods created specifically for athletes—sports drinks and energy bars—including a buyer's guide and the answer to a key question: Do the ingredients in these products pose any long-term health risks?

Nutrition for Cyclists will explain how your diet can improve your cycling performance. It discusses when and what to eat, whether you're at home, in a restaurant, or on a ride. It even reveals the best choices when making a midride convenience-store pit stop or shopping for a frozen, microwave dinner. And we'll tell you the keys to avoiding an upset stomach during cycling, as well as how to control your ravenous appetite after a long ride.

An entire section is devoted to those who would like to lose weight through cycling. Included is information developed exclusively for *Bicycling* and this book: an eight-week program to help you shed between 8 and 16 pounds while retaining the energy needed for strong riding, and a precise method for determining how many calories you burn on a given ride. Unlike other formulas, ours considers every key variable, including speed, hills, wind direction, and whether you ride alone or draft another cyclist.

To stay abreast of the latest research in cycling nutrition and new high-energy foods, we invite you to read *Bicycling*. It regularly contains articles by the sports nutrition experts listed in the credits on page 120, as well as others in this advancing field.

Ed Pavelka, Executive Editor
Bicycling Magazine

Part One

BASIC CONCEPTS

1 LESSONS FOR A NEW RIDER

Fred always participated in sports and, of course, he'd always eaten—but never at the same time. That is, until he became a cyclist. Cycling is the only sport (next to bowling) where eating and drinking are an integral part of the action. And the key factor isn't always what you eat, but how and when you eat it. As Fred learned the hard way, this can actually affect how well you ride.

He discovered this during his first day-long tour. He and his riding partners had covered approximately 25 miles in the Amish country surrounding Lancaster, Pennsylvania, when they stopped for lunch at a family-style restaurant. To the Pennsylvania Dutch, "family style" means heaping portions of ham loaf, fried chicken, roast beef, mashed potatoes, cottage cheese, apple butter, and cracker pudding, all passed from one stranger to the next across a communal table.

The food was great and Fred ate plenty, but as he waddled back to his bike he suddenly dreaded the remaining miles. What was supposed to be a pit stop had become a pig-out. He had made a terrible mistake.

Eat to Beat the Bonk

Phillip Harvey, Ph.D., a California nutritionist and cyclist, explains that "if too much food gets into your system too quickly, your digestive system has to compete against your muscles for blood." In Fred's case, this translated into an overloaded body that couldn't provide enough energy for hard riding while digesting gobs of cracker pudding.

Nevertheless, on any ride longer than 2 hours, you need to eat. Your body stores carbohydrate in the form of glycogen, which it later uses to fuel your muscles. You have enough naturally stored glycogen to provide energy for short rides, but not enough to last through a couple of hours of strenuous cycling. This will eventually lead to the exhaustion that cyclists fondly term "bonking."

According to Dr. Harvey, the best way to avoid the bonk is to constantly nibble while you ride. This means eating before you're hungry and drinking before you're thirsty to keep your energy level high and your body well hydrated. For long rides, eat about 60 to 90 minutes before leaving, about an hour into the ride, and steadily thereafter.

How to Eat and Ride

Just as important as when you eat is *how* you eat. Lon Haldeman, two-time winner of the Race Across America (RAAM), says, "Some people eat while riding no-handed, but I've never felt comfortable doing it. If it's food that won't melt, I'll keep it in my jersey pocket and just reach back and eat it one-handed. The more fatigued I get, the less I trust my judgment. Especially late in a ride, I'll always keep at least one hand on the bar (positioned near the stem for best control).

"Rolling terrain is the hardest place to eat," Haldeman continues. "You're either flying down a hill at 40 mph and it's not safe to have less than two hands on the bar, or you're on an uphill and climbing out of the saddle. If I know I'm coming to a long hilly stretch, I'll eat ahead of time." (To reduce the risk of stomach discomfort, eat at least 30 minutes before a lengthy, strenuous climb.)

What to Eat

Of course, *what* you put in your stomach is also important. Haldeman and fellow RAAM winner Pete Penseyres used a high-carbohydrate liquid diet during their May 1987 destruction of the transcontinental tandem record. This provided a steady source of easily accessible energy while preventing mood swings, drowsiness, and variations in performance. It also prevented dehydration, a common crippler of long-distance cyclists. In fact, Harvey says staying hydrated is of primary importance to all types of riders. He recommends drinking one bottle of water per hour, depending on the temperature and how much you perspire. You might even want to carry two bottles, one filled with water and the other with diluted fruit juice or a commercial sports drink to provide carbohydrate.

Regarding food, Harvey notes that "the average American diet is high in fat. If this is true in your case, you'll never have enough carbohydrate to keep the glycogen stores in your legs high. And there's nothing you can do about it once you're on the bike. It's like training—your endurance capacity depends on how well you've prepared."

To ready yourself, follow the basic tenets of good nutrition by eating a high-carbohydrate, low-fat diet. Include lots of fresh vegetables, and reduce your consumption of red meat.

On the road, eat portable carbohydrate-rich foods. Harvey suggests apples, fig bars, and oranges. And if you ever wondered why cycling jerseys have pockets in the back, Harvey offers this theory: "Bananas," he says. "Jerseys are set up perfectly for holding bananas."

Haldeman's mobile goodie list includes celery sticks, cashews, crackers, and (this sounds familiar) apples, fig bars, and bananas. "Bananas aren't hard to peel one-handed," he adds. "You just bite off the end and peel them with your teeth."

According to Haldeman, you know you're really proficient at eating on a bike when you can munch a granola bar despite a runny nose. "It's a mess," he says. "You're trying to chew and swallow this dry granola bar and there's no way you can get any air. You have to go about 15 seconds without breathing."

But that's better than all afternoon with a belly full of ham loaf.

2 EATING, DRINKING, AND CYCLING

Because most new riders are surprised to learn that eating is often an important part of cycling, let's get right to the reasons for it. In true journalistic style, here are the pertinent facts about the "why, when, what, and how" of eating, drinking, and riding.

Why You Need to Eat and Drink on the Bike

Food replenishes the energy burned while riding. We can't stress this enough, so for the sake of clarity let's quickly review what we discussed in chapter 1. Every time you eat something, your body takes the food's carbohydrate (natural compounds derived from starches and sugars) and stores it as fuel (glycogen) in your muscles. You have enough stored glycogen to provide energy for short rides. For longer efforts, however, you need to eat or your glycogen stores will become depleted. When this occurs, less fuel reaches your brain and muscles and you feel dizzy and tired. In cycling, this is known as bonking, which we mentioned earlier. In addition, cycling also results in fluid loss. To avoid dehydration and its debilitating effects, never leave home without a full water bottle.

When You Should Eat and Drink

While riding, drink before you're thirsty and eat before you're hungry. This rule is essential to health and performance, so we'll review it several times in this book. If you wait for your body to tell you it needs nourishment, the energy won't be able to reach your muscles fast enough to help. One rule of thumb is to take a big swig from your water bottle every 15 minutes. You should consume about 20 ounces (the contents of one standard-size bottle) of liquid per hour. Drink more if it's hot and humid. Another rule is to allow yourself about an hour for digestion before riding. If you'll be cycling for more than 90 minutes, nibble periodically during the ride. Avoid large midride meals. Your digestive system requires lots of blood to process such meals, which leaves less for delivering oxygen to your muscles.

What You Should Eat and Drink

For fluid replacement on short rides, water is excellent. Commercial sports drinks such as Body Fuel and Exceed are preferred by many cyclists for longer rides. This is because they replenish lost liquid and glycogen stores and are easier for the body to process than solids. According to studies, cyclists can ride nearly one-third farther when ingesting a sports drink.

Perhaps the most popular on-bike food is the banana. It's easy to eat, provides 105 calories of carbohydrate, and replaces potassium, an important element lost via sweating. Other fresh fruit such as pears (98 calories) and apples (81 calories) also provide carbohydrate, vitamins, minerals, and water—all necessary for strong cycling. Avoid high-fat treats such as candy while riding. Fat is an ineffective fuel source compared to carbohydrate. Researchers report that when you're burning fat for energy, you can reach only 50 to 60 percent of your aerobic potential.

Many long-distance cyclists mix nuts, raisins, whole grain or enriched cereal, and other favorites into a personalized concoction called "gorp" (good ol' raisins and peanuts). This delivers a steady flow of carbohydrate and is easy to nibble.

Caffeine (coffee, cola, tea) may give you a significant boost, but it also encourages fluid loss through urination. Since riding also reduces fluid levels, try to avoid a significant dose of caffeine. In any case, research shows caffeine's uplifting effects decrease once you become a routine user.

When off your bike, your diet should be 60 to 70 percent carbohydrate, 20 to 30 percent fat, and 10 to 15 percent protein. High-carbo foods include fruit, pasta, potatoes, whole grain breads, and vegetables.

How to Eat While Riding

The best place to store food while riding is in the rear pocket of your jersey. To reach it, first grip the handlebar with one hand near the stem to hold the bike steady. Then reach around with the other hand to grab that banana, which you can peel with your teeth and eat. Another approach is to snack during rest stops. It's common for cyclists to stash food in seat or handlebar bags for devouring at spontaneous roadside picnics.

Finally, don't forget the postride meal. As a cyclist, you'll regularly burn hundreds if not thousands of calories while exercising. So when you get home, enjoy an extra helping of your favorite carbohydrate-rich food. This is a reward that will also restock your energy stores for tomorrow's ride.

■3 FUEL FOR SPRING TRAINING

Each spring, as the days get longer, the weather gets warmer, and it's almost time to start amassing some serious road mileage, don't forget one important nutritional nugget. Namely, that at this time of year as your cycling increases, it's crucial to adjust your diet.

Increase Your Calories

With more training, you'll need more calories. But you shouldn't just increase your food intake indiscriminately. You need to eat the right stuff: carbohydrate. If you don't eat enough of it, your body won't be able to store enough muscle glycogen (your body's preferred fuel for aerobic exercise). And if training depletes your glycogen, you'll feel listless and light-headed on the bike. In other words, you'll "bonk."

Most cyclists think muscle glycogen depletion can occur only on long rides. For the most part this is true, and it's the reason you need to eat during rides lasting 2 hours or more. However, glycogen depletion can occur more gradually, taking place over several days of short rides. Each day that you don't replace all the glycogen used in training, your glycogen stores decrease a bit. As a result, each successive workout becomes more difficult and less enjoyable, and after a few days you will find it harder to maintain your normal intensity. Even short, easy workouts will make you feel fatigued. In addition, you may suddenly lose several pounds due to glycogen and water loss.

This condition, known as training glycogen depletion, occurs so often that most athletes don't consider it unusual. They think it's normal to be tired after several days of workouts. However, while you can expect general fatigue after riding, it isn't normal to be consistently tired and unable to repeat your past performance. When this happens, it's probably your diet that's at fault.

Fortunately, it's a problem that's easy to correct. By increasing your carbohydrate intake and sprinkling your riding schedule with rest days, you can prevent training glycogen depletion. A carbo-rich diet allows you to maintain adequate glycogen stores. The rest days give your muscles time to recover and rebuild these stores.

Put Carbohydrate in Your Diet

Carbohydrate, which is essential for glycogen synthesis, should account for at least 60 percent of your total calories. The typical American diet, however, is only 46 percent carbohydrate. A high-carb diet (70 percent of total calories or more) can restore muscle glycogen to normal levels in 24 hours. This allows you to maintain endurance even during successive days of intense training.

What type of carbohydrate, or "carbo," is best? There are basically two kinds: complex and refined. Complex carbos include fruits, vegetables, whole grain breads and cereals, rice, pasta, and beans. Refined carbos are sugars and sweets such as candy, cake, and soda. During the first 24 hours after exhaustive exercise, there's no difference in glycogen synthesis between the two types of carbohydrate. But after a day, complex carbohydrate promotes significantly greater glycogen synthesis than refined carbohydrate. Complex carbo also provides general health advantages since it offers fiber and nutrients with its calories.

Don't Overdo

In spring, it's also tempting to use increased training as an excuse for indiscriminate eating. However, this is a proven recipe for weight gain. While you should increase your food intake some-what, don't overdo it. One way to avoid gaining weight in spring is to eat fewer empty calories—foods that are high in fat, sugar, and alcohol.

Your body tends to store these calories as fat. Conversely, carbohydrate calories are harder to convert to fat and are more likely to be burned for energy. This doesn't mean you can eat as many carbohydrate calories as you want and not gain weight. It does mean it will take more excess carbohydrate calories than fat calories to cause weight gain.

Be a Fat Miser

Fat is present in dairy products, such as cheese, ice cream, and whole milk, as well as meat, eggs, nuts, and fried foods. Other dietary sources of fat are more obvious: margarine, butter, mayonnaise, salad dressing, oil, and sour cream. You can decrease your fat intake by selecting low-fat dairy products and protein foods (such as chicken, fish, and beans) and limiting your use of fatty spreads and dressings.

Also try to decrease your sugar intake by eating less cake, cookies, pies, and candy. Replace soft drinks with diet sodas, and use sugar substitutes. Remember, too, that alcoholic beverages are high in calories and low in nutrients. If you drink alcohol, compensate by decreasing your intake of other fat and sugar sources.

By following these recommendations, you'll have more energy for early-season riding, and you'll reap added fitness benefits later in the year.

4 BUILDING YOUR ENDURANCE AND BEATING THE BONK

You've been riding for several hours, feeling great and enjoying the scenery. But for the past 15 minutes your riding partner has been talking continuously, and it's beginning to irritate you. Halfway up the next hill, you reach for the shift lever and discover that you're already in your lowest gear. You struggle toward the top, where your partner is waiting with a curious look on his face.

"What's the jerk smiling about?" you wonder. "This is a stupid ride, anyway. I should have stayed home and mowed the lawn."

Wait a minute. What's going on here? A few minutes ago you felt great, now you feel terrible. Why? Simply put, you've "bonked."

It's a humorous word that's traditional in cycling, and that's why you've already encountered it in this book. But it's never funny when it happens. In fact, bonking is such a miserable experience that avoiding it must become a primary objective of your cycling nutrition. On any long ride, much of what you eat and when you eat it should be geared toward fending off the bonk's drastic consequences. Let's find out exactly what causes it and what you can do to prevent it.

What's Happening to Your Energy?

Bonk describes the symptoms that occur when your body's essential carbohydrate stores are depleted as a result of sustained exercise. As you ride, most of the fuel being oxidized, or burned, is consumed by your active muscles. Both fat and carbohydrate can be utilized for this process. Fat, stored in fatty tissue, is reduced to free fatty acids and transported by the blood to the working muscles. In contrast, carbohydrate is stored within the muscles as glycogen, which is a long polymer composed of many glucose molecules. During exercise, individual molecules are removed from the polymer and used as energy.

However, your vital organs also require a continuous supply of fuel. Whether at rest or during exercise, your brain and nervous system, for instance, depend upon blood glucose. The reason for this dependence is that the cells of your nervous system don't store glycogen and can't use fat. Thus, to meet energy requirements, your blood glucose levels must be tightly regulated and maintained. This job is largely done by your liver, which contains large stores of glycogen that can be converted to glucose.

With the muscles and organs vying for glucose, extended exertion can drain the liver. When blood glucose levels become too low to meet the fuel requirements of your central nervous system, you begin feeling disoriented, tired, irritated, and generally miserable. In a word, you bonk.

A Quick Solution

Fortunately, you can remedy the bonk. When your blood glucose levels fall as a result of liver glycogen depletion, you can replenish them by simply eating or drinking something rich in carbohydrate. This is quickly digested into simple sugars that enter the bloodstream and are transported to the liver, muscles, and other organs.

Even better, you can avoid bonking in the first place by periodically eating or drinking small amounts of carbohydrate while riding. This will enable your stomach to continuously add glucose to the blood. In turn, this will greatly reduce the drain on your liver's valuable glycogen stores. The trick is to begin eating or drinking about 15 minutes into a long ride and continue to do so every 10 to 15 minutes thereafter.

Of course, eating on short rides isn't necessary. But how you define "short" and "long" depends on your fitness. For novices, an hour-long ride is very long. For veterans, 2 hours might be short. A good preventive measure in any case is to never leave home without your favorite energy food and/or drink—just in case.

When Your Muscles
Hit the Wall

Interestingly, although bonking and "hitting the wall" are terms that are often used interchangeably, there is a difference. Both result from fuel depletion. However, unlike bonking, which is caused by the depletion of liver glycogen, hitting the wall stems from the depletion of *muscle* glycogen. Bonking is avoidable and curable. Hitting the wall can be delayed by ingesting carbohydrate, but once it happens, you're essentially finished for the day.

Hitting the wall is terminal to your training because as the rate of fuel consumption rises in response to intensifying exercise, the muscles turn to their most readily available fuel—muscle glycogen. In fact, it's the only fuel that can support exercise at levels greater than 70 percent of your VO_2 max (your measure of maximum aerobic ability). When you run out of muscle glycogen, you're only able to exercise at very moderate intensity.

(Another reason muscle glycogen is so important is that it provides an essential intermediate product that's required to burn fat.)

As with beating the bonk, the key to avoiding the wall is maintaining a steady intake of carbohydrate. Another trick is to not waste the muscle glycogen you have. For instance, each time you accelerate rapidly on the bike, your body switches to an anaerobic metabolism to meet the extra energy demands. This process—which is so demanding that your body can't take in enough oxygen—uses glycogen much less efficiently than aerobic metabolism. Therefore, on long rides, always accelerate smoothly, avoid blasting up hills, concentrate on your breathing, and don't be tempted into riding harder than usual.

The Best Carbo Sources

Two rich sources of carbohydrate during rides are sports drinks and energy bars. These can be purchased in most bike shops. Experiment with different brands until you find ones that taste good and work for you. Also, there are many common, less expensive alternatives, including fig cookies, fruit bars, bananas, dried fruit, and granola bars. As with energy drinks, experiment with different solid foods. Most riders settle on a combination of solid and liquid supplements.

Whatever you select, remember to use it. You'd be amazed how many experienced riders bonk or hit the wall with their pockets full of food. By sipping and nibbling every 10 to 15 minutes, you'll be able to avoid the bonk. And when the ride is over, you may even feel like mowing the lawn.

Part Two
THE RIGHT THINGS TO EAT

5 THE GOOD STUFF: CARBOHYDRATE

When you reach into your jersey for a banana during a ride, that piece of fruit begins a journey more fascinating and magical than even the greatest bicycle tour. By the end of its trip, that banana—or sandwich or cookie or whatever you ate—is transformed into energy, the key to completing *your* journey.

How Food Turns into Energy

Along the way, several interesting changes occur. Edward F. Coyle, Ph.D., a cyclist and leading carbohydrate researcher, chronicles these alterations. He lives in a fascinating world of questions: Should you eat before a ride? How can food and drink combat fatigue during a century? What type of riding is best for losing weight? How concentrated should a sports drink be? To what extent can food and drink extend endurance?

The process begins with a piece of food and the three main compounds it contains: protein, carbohydrate, and fat.

Your body breaks down the energy stored in the molecules of the food, says Dr. Coyle, the director of the human performance laboratory at the University of Texas at Austin and a member of *Bicycling*'s fitness advisory board. Protein is rarely used for energy, but it does play other crucial roles in your body. Carbohydrate, on the other hand, is the preferred source of energy because your body can break it down faster than fat. Therefore, it rapidly releases the energy you need for a vigorous ride.

Dietary fat, however, is a *stored* energy source, either in your blood as free fatty acids, in your muscle fiber, or beneath your skin. You burn more body fat on long, slow rides, which is why such efforts are often recommended for losing weight. According to Dr. Coyle, however, this logic is flawed. He contends that an hour of slow riding *will* burn fat, but when you eat later, the calories you consume will only replenish these fat stores. A better weight-loss approach, therefore, is to burn as many calories as you can by riding hard. In any case, no matter how you look at it, fat is the body's secondary fuel source.

Fat Is a Poor Fuel

When your body is forced to use fat as an energy source, you are limited to exercising at no more than 50 to 60 percent of your aerobic capacity, says Dr. Coyle. For instance, if you can normally maintain 24 mph, you won't be able to ride much faster than 15 mph for more than 5 to 10 minutes. Fat obviously is a limiting source of energy. Consider that if you're on a fairly intense ride, maintaining a heart rate of 150 to 160 beats per minute, you get only about 40 percent of your energy from fat. The rest comes from carbohydrate—your body's fuel of choice.

Build Glycogen Stores

As carbohydrate—a natural compound coming from starches and sugars—travels through your digestive system, it is converted into its storage status, known as glycogen. Then it takes one of two paths. Some carbohydrate goes to the liver, where it's converted into glucose, a principal energy source of living organisms. This quickly enters the circulatory system as blood glucose. Meanwhile, other carbohydrate is stored in the muscles as muscle glycogen. This process, however, occurs at a much slower rate. (We discussed blood glucose and muscle glycogen in chapter 4, where we covered "the bonk" and "hitting the wall.")

Early in a ride, you rely almost exclusively upon muscle glycogen for energy, explains Dr. Coyle. But as your muscle glycogen levels decline, you rely more on blood glucose. In just 3 hours of riding, the percentage of carbohydrate energy coming from muscle glycogen steadily declines from 100 percent to zero, while energy from blood glucose increases from zero to 100 percent.

After a few hours of pedaling without food, your glycogen and glucose stores will be depleted. Even if you have ample fat stores, the process through which these are converted to energy is not efficient enough to sustain your riding effort. With less fuel reaching your brain and muscles, you'll begin to feel dizzy and fatigued. Eventually, you'll bonk.

Carbo: The Ultimate Fuel

But what if you had been ingesting carbo-rich food and liquid during the ride? Could such feedings replenish your blood glucose stores fast enough to forestall the bonk?

Until recently, the scientific consensus was no—carbohydrate feedings don't contribute significant energy for exercise. The thinking was that you shouldn't bother with sports drinks because they couldn't be used rapidly enough by the body. But Dr. Coyle and others are finding that this theory isn't correct. "The body can use carbohydrate during the latter stages of exercise when muscle glycogen is very low," he says. "We tested cyclists between the third and fourth hour of a ride and found they weren't using any muscle glycogen. All their carbohydrate energy was coming from the glucose they were drinking."

Dr. Coyle has shown that if cyclists eat and drink while riding, they can extend their endurance, despite the fact that their muscle glycogen is exhausted. In one study, he had two groups of cyclists ride to exhaustion, then ingest either a placebo or carbohydrate. When they resumed riding 20 minutes later, those who ingested the carbohydrate were able to cycle 45 minutes longer.

Normally, if you start to fatigue, the end of your riding energy comes quickly. You bonk and it's over, explains Dr. Coyle. But with steady carbohydrate feeding, you fatigue, but you're still able to grind it out.

Carbo and Sports Drinks

Having determined and demonstrated the effectiveness of carbohydrate feeding, Dr. Coyle has turned to dispelling some other myths.

For instance, experts used to believe that a sports drink should not contain more than 2.5 percent carbohydrate. It was thought that anything more would slow the solution's passage from the stomach to the intestines. This would have two negative effects. First, it would take longer for the body to absorb the fluid, thus inhibiting its ability to cool itself via sweating. Second, such slow emptying would cause nausea.

Dr. Coyle agrees that high concentrations of carbohydrate can slow gastric emptying, but disagrees about the consequences.

"The stomach can empty a liter of water per hour, but it can only empty 800 milliliters per hour of a 5 percent carbohydrate solution," he explains. "Statistically, this is significant. But functionally, it doesn't constitute a big difference. No one has been able to prove that the slowdown in gastric emptying makes any difference in the body's ability to cool itself."

In fact, some recent studies have shown the opposite. A research group at Ball State University in Muncie, Indiana, compared the effects of ingesting 5, 6, and 7 percent solutions during a long ride. The tests resulted in an extended performance for each rider who participated. Meanwhile, a University of South Carolina study compared 6 and 12 percent solutions. This one was conducted at 91-degree temperatures to gauge the effect on sweating. The 12 percent dose did not alter the body's ability to cool itself. However, it did cause some upset stomachs.

Indeed, nausea is the main reason extremely high concentrations are still not universally accepted. When Dr. Coyle fed cyclists a 10 percent carbohydrate solution, 10 percent of the subjects vomited. "When you start ingesting solutions that have 7 to 10 percent or more carbohydrate, it can build up in the stomach and cause gastric distress," he explains. "But it's very individual. Some people can tolerate any concentration and empty it quickly. The key is to experiment to find what's best for you."

Dr. Coyle notes that during exercise, the body can draw glucose from the blood at the rate of 1 gram per minute, or 60 grams per hour. Thus, to be effective, an energy drink should deliver between 40 and 60 grams of carbohydrate per hour. To accomplish this, you can either drink a little of a very concentrated solution or a lot of a diluted solution. Doing the latter will also help you meet your fluid replacement needs. However, with a 2.5 percent solution, you'd have to drink several liters per hour, which isn't realistic.

TABLE 5–1.
Carbohydrate Calorie Counter

Food	Portion	Calories
Cereal		
Cheerios	1¼ cups	111
Corn Chex	1 cup	111
Rice Chex	1⅛ cups	112
Shredded Wheat w/fruit	½ cup	100
Wheat Chex	⅔ cup	104
Cookies and Crackers		
Animal crackers	15	120
Fruit bars, raisin-filled biscuits	1	53
Gingersnaps	7	115
Graham crackers	4	120
Vanilla wafers	7	130
Fruit		
Apples		
Fresh	1	81
Dried	¼ cup	52
Apricots, dried	¼ cup	78
Banana	1	105
Blueberries	1 cup	82
Figs	¼ cup	127
Grapes	½ cup	57
Orange	1	62
Peaches, dried	¼ cup	96
Pears		
Fresh	1	98
Dried	¼ cup	118
Prunes	¼ cup	96
Raisins	¼ cup	109

Food	Portion	Calories
Raspberries	1 cup	61
Strawberries	1 cup	45
Miscellaneous		
Bagel, plain	1	160–200
Fruit roll-up	1 (½ oz.)	50
Pita bread w/sliced fruit or shredded vegetables, plain or w/ small amount of low-calorie dressing		165

SOURCE: Compiled by Liz Applegate, Ph.D., and Diane Drabinsky, R.D.

Photograph 5–1. Foods for the road.

The New Word
on Eating While You Ride

Another bit of dated logic contends that eating carbo-rich foods immediately before a ride stimulates the secretion of insulin, a hormone that actually removes glucose from the blood. When combined with exercise, this can result in a dramatic drop in blood glucose, a condition called hypoglycemia. The symptoms include cold sweat, headache, confusion, hallucinations, convulsions, and even coma. At the very least, it's said the scarcity of glucose leads to light-headedness and lower performance. But Dr. Coyle sees it differently.

"It's overrated. Most riders never sense it," he says. "We've found that fewer than 25 percent of those who experience hypoglycemia ever have a central nervous system effect where they feel shaky or irritable. Early in a ride, it's of almost no consequence. Only 1 in 30 people notices the effects. Later, they'll notice the depletion of blood glucose because they're depriving their muscles of energy. At this point, they may be able to tolerate the effects of hypoglycemia, but they can't tolerate the fact that their legs lack energy."

By ingesting carbohydrate throughout the ride, Dr. Coyle continues, you're providing the muscles with extra energy, so you're able to ride longer.

Fatigue

But why, you might wonder, can't you just keep ingesting carbohydrate and cycle indefinitely?

"Nobody knows," says Dr. Coyle. "We've studied cyclists riding with low levels of muscle glycogen but high levels of blood glucose. Their muscles seemed to be taking in glucose adequately. But after extending the exercise for about an hour, they had a second fatigue and they stopped. Something else is going on other than carbohydrate. We just don't know what."

A study at the University of Waterloo, Ontario, has also concluded that other unknown factors, not carbohydrate availability, cause fatigue. One suspect is an electrical change within the muscles.

But even if science can't as yet enable you to pedal indefinitely, you can improve your cycling performance and extend endurance by using carbohydrate correctly, especially on glycogen-depleting rides of 3 hours or more. For instance:

- A few days before a ride: "Ingest 600 grams of carbohydrate per day," says Dr. Coyle. This will have your glycogen stores brimming. To achieve this, you may want to try one of several commercial carbo-loaders on the market. These foodstuffs are designed to augment glycogen stores.
- A few hours before a ride: "It doesn't make much difference what you eat," says Dr. Coyle, "as long as you've eaten well the previous few days and the night before."
- During a ride: "On any ride longer than 3 hours," says Dr. Coyle, "bring bagels, a sports drink—anything high in carbohydrate. Liquids are easier to consume and provide necessary fluid. I suggest a carbohydrate concentration between 5 and 10 percent in volumes of 200 to 400 milliliters every 15 minutes." (A standard water bottle holds 590 milliliters.)

"But don't ignore solid food," he continues. "All carbohydrate is treated the same way by your body. In fact, it's good to mix solids with fluids, especially on long rides. I work with cycling teams and provide them with all types of carbohydrate fluid alternatives during races and hard rides. But once they've been riding about 6 hours, they all say the same thing: 'I want something solid.' "

Next time, offer a banana, and let the real ride begin.

6 THE IDEAL CYCLING DIET

It's no coincidence: The same foods that prevent heart disease, stroke, and cancer also enhance cycling.

You'll hear it frequently because it's so true: A high-carbohydrate, low-fat diet does it all. It fortifies you for consecutive days of training while increasing your odds of a long, healthy life. However, what you don't always hear is exactly how cyclists should use such a diet for their training and riding.

For example, avoid eating several hours before riding. This ensures that your stomach will be empty and that you won't become nauseated. Actually, a preride meal isn't a major source of energy for short rides. Your real fuel comes from the energy stores you've built with your daily diet. (For long rides, it's important to eat and drink while riding, of course.)

Two Types of Carbo

The best way to build and replenish your energy stores is with carbohydrate. Both the complex and simple (sugar) types of

TABLE 6–1.
Carbo-Training

Food	Portion	Carbohydrate (g)	Calories	Calories from Carbohydrate (%)
Fruit juice	1 cup	30	120	100
Dried fruit (raisins, apricots)	⅓ cup	40	160	100
Corn on the cob	1 ear	29	120	95
Banana	1 large	27	115	94
Baked potato	1 large	51	220	93
Rice, white cooked	1 cup	50	223	90
Cereal, flakes, w/out milk	1 cup	25	110	90
Spaghetti, cooked	1 cup	34	160	85
Corn grits, cooked	1 cup	31	146	85

carbohydrate supply your body with glycogen—the most efficient muscle fuel for cycling, as discussed in earlier chapters. But complex carbo (fruit, vegetables, beans, and whole grain breads and cereals) also offers several specific health advantages. The soluble fiber in oats, beans, and fruit reduces blood cholesterol. The insoluble fiber in wheat bran, whole grain products, and vegetables (particularly the skin) maintains healthy bowels. And fruits and vegetables rich in vitamin C and beta-carotene protect against certain types of cancer. For these reasons, as well as your performance needs, complex carbos should comprise about half of your daily caloric intake. Table 6-1 below lists some of the best carbohydrate sources.

Food	Portion	Carbohydrate (g)	Calories	Calories from Carbohydrate (%)
Kashi, cooked	1 cup	38	177	84
Wheat bulgur, cooked	1 cup	47	227	83
English muffin	1	30	150	80
Rice cakes	5	40	200	80
Pita bread	1 pocket	21	106	79
Popcorn, plain	4 cups	18	92	78
Bread sticks	4	30	154	78
Pancakes	3 (4″)	51	260	78
Pretzels, low-salt	2 oz.	43	222	77
Bagel	1	31	160	77
Kidney beans, canned	1 cup	35	186	75
Bread	2 slices	30	160	75

Source: *Runner's World*, September 1990.

Conversely, simple carbs should constitute less than 10 percent of your daily diet. Be careful about eating sweets such as cake and candy before riding. As discussed in chapter 5, the hormone insulin, which is secreted by the pancreas to counteract the influx of sugar, may lower blood sugar levels too much for some riders. This can cause weakness and light-headedness while riding.

Two Types of Fat

Just as there are two types of carbohydrate, there are two kinds of fat, saturated and unsaturated. Saturated fat, such as butter, is solid at room temperature and is derived mainly from animals (with the exception of palm and coconut oils, which are highly saturated vegetable fats). Unsaturated fat, such as corn oil, is liquid at room temperature and is derived mainly from plants.

A high-fat diet, particularly when the fat is saturated, increases blood cholesterol—a major risk factor for heart disease. It also increases the risk of certain types of cancer. Both the American Heart Association and the National Cancer Institute recommend that no more than 30 percent of your calories come from fat. Yet many Americans take in much more.

For a cyclist, this can be especially disastrous. You need to maintain your muscle glycogen stores by fueling up on complex carbos, and this can't be done on a high-fat diet. The body's slow digestion of fat can also make you sluggish (carbohydrate is digested much faster). If you ride 1 hour a day, about 60 percent of your calories should be derived from carbohydrate. If you ride several hours a day, make it 70 percent. This will ensure that your glycogen stores are full.

A Word on Protein

While fat and carbohydrate receive most of the attention, there's also another important food compound: protein. The body uses it chiefly for tissue growth and repair. Your diet should be 10 to 15 percent protein. If you consume more than you need, it'll either be used for energy or turned into body fat. Excess protein can also contribute to dehydration, since your kidneys need more water to process it. Dehydration can impair your cycling performance, even for rides as short as an hour.

Sample Diets

To achieve a balanced diet and make sure of having the energy needed for cycling, try the following recommended menus for low- and high-mileage riders.

If You Ride an Hour or Less a Day . . .

Men should eat 2,000 calories, of which 57 percent come from carbohydrate, 29 percent from fat, and 14 percent from protein.

Breakfast: ⅓ cup bran cereal; 1 cup low-fat milk; 1 banana; 1 slice raisin toast; ½ cup grapefruit juice.

Lunch: Tuna melt (use a nonstick vegetable spray on grill) made with 2 slices whole wheat bread, 3 ounces tuna mixed with 1 teaspoon mayonnaise, celery, green onion, 1 ounce Cheddar cheese, and 1 tomato slice; carrot and celery sticks; 1 cup apple juice; 1 cup low-fat yogurt with 1 cup raspberries.

Dinner: Stir-fry made with 2 teaspoons peanut oil, 4 ounces skinned chicken, and 1½ cups vegetables; 1½ cups brown rice; 1 orange.

Snack: 1 cup low-fat milk and 1 medium blueberry muffin.

Women should eat 1,500 calories of which 56 percent come from carbohydrate, 27 percent from fat, and 17 percent from protein.

Breakfast: 1 cup Cream of Wheat with 2 tablespoons raisins; ½ cup orange juice.

Lunch: Sandwich made with ½ whole grain pita bread, ⅓ cup seasoned garbanzo beans, lettuce, tomato slice, and onion; ½ cup cooked broccoli; ½ mango; 1 cup low-fat milk.

Dinner: 4 ounces lean beef; baked potato with 2 teaspoons margarine; ½ cup spinach salad with 1 tablespoon French dressing; yogurt shake made with 1 cup low-fat yogurt, ½ banana, and ¼ cup strawberries.

If You Ride 2 or More Hours a Day . . .

Men should eat 3,000 calories, of which 69 percent come from carbohydrate, 18 percent from fat, and 13 percent from protein.

Breakfast: 1 cup orange juice; 1 cup oatmeal with sliced banana; 1 cup low-fat milk; two slices wheat bread with 2 teaspoons margarine.

Lunch: Sandwich made with 2 slices rye bread, 3 ounces turkey, 1 ounce mozzarella cheese, lettuce, 1 tomato slice, and 1 teaspoon mayonnaise; 1 cup apple juice; 1 orange; 1 cup lemon sherbet.

Snack: 8 graham crackers; 1 cup low-fat milk; 1 apple.

Dinner: 2 cups spaghetti with ⅔ cup tomato sauce, mushrooms, and 2 tablespoons Parmesan cheese; 4 slices french bread with 2 teaspoons margarine; ½ cup broccoli; ½ cup ice cream with ¾ cup strawberries.

Snack: 6 cups air-popped popcorn.

Women should eat 2,500 calories, of which 70 percent come from carbohydrate, 16 percent from fat, and 14 percent from protein.

Breakfast: 1 cup grapefruit juice; 1 cup Cream of Wheat with ½ cup blueberries; 1 cup low-fat milk; 2 slices wheat bread with 2 teaspoons margarine.

Lunch: Sandwich made with 2 slices wheat bread, 3 ounces lean beef, 1 ounce Jack cheese, lettuce, 1 tomato slice, and mustard; 1 cup grape juice; 1 orange; 1 cup orange sherbet.

Snack: 4 graham crackers; 1 cup low-fat milk; 1 apple.

Dinner: 2 cups spaghetti with ⅔ cup tomato sauce, mushrooms, and 2 tablespoons Parmesan cheese; 2 slices french bread (easy on the margarine); ½ cup broccoli; ½ cup ice cream with ¾ cup strawberries.

Snack: 3 cups air-popped popcorn.

▪7▪ LIQUID ENERGY

Just a few years ago, sports drinks didn't exist. Back in the 1970s—believe it or not—recreational athletes drank plain water. And get this: For energy, they ate food!

Water? Food? Imagine.

Today, cyclists have gone beyond such primitive, albeit effective, practices. A variety of specially formulated sports drinks is available. Each supplies carbohydrate while also replacing minerals (electrolytes) and fluid lost through sweating. Indeed, such high-tech concoctions have become the drink of choice for many cyclists. A 1989 survey of *Bicycling* readers found that 62 percent sometimes use a sports drink.

So, will putting H_2O in your water bottle soon be as passé as wearing wool shorts? Is the banana destined to become a relic of the past?

Well, maybe not yet, but sports drinks certainly merit your consideration. They're the most convenient way to give yourself a steady supply of energy during a ride.

How They Work

Sports drinks typically contain some form of carbohydrate (glucose, sucrose, glucose polymer) along with minerals and artificial flavoring. Their simple formulation allows them to travel through the digestive system faster than regular food. Thus, they can be used for energy quicker.

In addition, sports drinks hydrate the body as fast as water. It was previously believed that such mixtures lingered in the stomach, so if you relied solely on a sports drink for fluid replacement, you might dehydrate. However, recent studies have shown no difference in the time it takes a sports drink or water to enter the bloodstream. In most cases this means there's no need to also consume water when using a commercial drink. Nevertheless, these drinks can taste syrupy as they warm, so most riders carry a bottle of water, too.

Concentrated Energy Boosters

To be most effective, a sports drink must contain the proper amount of carbohydrate. If it's too concentrated, the fluid won't be absorbed into the bloodstream fast enough. Instead, it'll stay in the stomach, causing nausea, cramps, and sometimes diarrhea, as discussed in chapter 5. Conversely, if the drink doesn't have enough carbohydrate, it'll be absorbed easily, but it won't provide enough of an energy boost.

For most riders, the ideal concentration is 5 to 8 percent carbohydrate (5 to 8 grams of carbohydrate for each 100 grams of fluid). The mixing instructions on most sports drinks produce a concentration in this range. Juices and sodas, on the other hand, are more than 10 percent carbohydrate. When consumed in the large quantities necessary to avoid dehydration, these drinks may cause stomach distress if not diluted with water.

Some elite endurance athletes, such as Race Across America veterans Pete Penseyres and Lon Haldeman, use sports drinks with carbohydrate concentrations as high as 25 percent. But their energy needs and physiological abilities are extremely high. In addition, they've become accustomed to concentrations that would cause stomach problems for most other riders.

Different Drinks, Different Carbos

On rides lasting less than 2 hours, water is all you need because your existing fuel stores contain ample energy. But on longer rides, these stores will become depleted. When this happens, you need efficient fuel in a hurry. And this is what a sports drink gives you. Study after study has shown that the ingestion of such drinks improves endurance.

But does the type of carbohydrate in the drink make a difference? It's been touted that glucose polymer drinks such as Exceed and Body Fuel enter the bloodstream even faster than the usual sucrose- or glucose-based mixtures. (Glucose polymer drinks contain chains of glucose molecules rather than individual molecules.) However, a study conducted in 1986 at the University of Iowa compared the effects of a 10 percent glucose solution and a 10 percent glucose polymer mixture and found no significant differences.

Replacing Electrolytes

On long rides, you must also be concerned with replacing electrolytes. These are minerals (sodium, chloride, potassium) that carry an electrical charge that's necessary for muscle contraction and the maintenance of fluid levels. If you don't use a sports drink (or don't eat) on a long ride, you can suffer dangerous electrolyte imbalances such as a low blood sodium condition called hyponatremia.

This condition is caused by losing sodium when you sweat, then diluting what remains in the bloodstream by drinking only water. If this happens, you will feel lethargic, confused, and weak. Fortunately, this doesn't occur often and you can prevent it by consuming a sports drink.

Before and After a Ride

After a ride, sports drinks replenish lost nutrients and restore fluid levels more effectively than water. In addition, there's a class of high-calorie, high-carbohydrate sports drinks (Carboplex, Carbo Plus, Exceed High Carbohydrate Source, Gatorlode) specifically designed for building carbo supplies before a ride and restoring them afterward. However, these are so concentrated that they aren't recommended for use during cycling because they can cause an upset stomach.

Of course, although it might be outmoded, you could still load up on carbohydrate the old-fashioned way with a heaping plate of solid, nondrinkable pasta.

8 FILLING YOUR "INNER TUBE"

Here is a list of some of the best foods for cycling, especially if you're touring. All are easy to carry and eat while riding or at rest stops. Simply pack them in plastic bags, and you're ready to go!

Fresh fruit: Provides water, carbohydrate, vitamins, minerals. Good source of fiber. Bananas (105 calories) and oranges (62 calories) replace potassium lost in sweating.

Dried fruit: Light, keeps well. Concentrated source of carbohydrate and potassium. Figs (48 calories) provide calcium, iron, and fiber. Apricots (17 calories) are rich in vitamin A.

Sports drinks: Replace lost body fluid and supply easily absorbed carbohydrate. For most brands, about 175 calories per standard, 20-ounce water bottle. Studies report cyclists ride faster and nearly one-third farther when using them. Plain water, of course, is also good for replenishing body fluid. Drink at least one water bottle per hour when riding.

Energy bars: About 200 calories. Vitamins, minerals, good taste, high carbohydrate. Light, need no refrigeration. Brands differ in fat and protein content, so check labels. Avoid chocolate coatings in hot weather.

Bagel: 160 calories. Excellent source of complex carbohydrate, which is necessary for replenishing glycogen stores. Packs easily, needs no refrigeration, sturdier than bread.

Photograph 8–1. Energy boosters.

Peanut butter sandwich: 315 calories. High in protein, fat, and carbohydrate. Easily made, needs no refrigeration.

Gorp: Acronym for good ol' raisins and peanuts. 300 calories per half cup. Personalize the mix with M&M's, dried fruit, or nuts. Easy to eat while riding. Allows for steady calorie intake throughout the day.

Macaroni: 190 calories per cooked, 1-cup serving. Light, easily made, good source of complex carbohydrate and B vitamins.

Dried soup: 80 calories per cup. Replaces sodium and lost fluid. Light, easily cooked. Add vegetables, noodles, and the like.

Freeze-dried meals: 200 calories per 1-cup serving. Good emergency rations.

Cereal: 100 calories per 1-ounce serving. Whole grain and enriched cereals contain B vitamins, minerals, and fiber. Granola has more fat than regular cereal.

9 FIVE "RECIPES" FOR SPECIAL OCCASIONS

Different types of rides require different types of nutritional preparation. If you eat for a century as you would for an interval workout, or vice versa, you'll be in trouble. Each type of ride has its own list of nutritional do's and don'ts. Here, sports nutritionist Elizabeth Applegate, Ph.D., explains all the rules, including how, what, and when to eat for the five most common types of rides.

Commute

Intensity: steady speed, light to moderate effort
Distance: 5 to 20 miles
Time: less than 90 minutes

In preparing nutritionally for a commute, you should have two goals: to ride comfortably, and to have enough energy left to do your job or schoolwork.

Eating a preride meal is important. For morning commutes, have a high-carbohydrate breakfast that includes fruit, cereal, skim milk, and whole grain bread or muffins. For lunch or an afternoon snack, eat nutritional foods such as pasta, fruits, and vegetables so your glycogen stores are fully replenished for the ride home. Avoid eating sugary foods an hour before cycling if you find that they create fatiguing changes in your blood sugar level.

However, never let your commuting get in the way of maintaining a balanced diet. For example, don't purposely avoid foods rich in protein. This can lead to long-term performance problems and dangerously affect your health.

In general, give yourself 30 to 45 minutes to digest your meal before you begin pedaling. Caffeine (coffee, tea, or cola) might give you that get-up-and-go feeling, but it's also a diuretic. Large amounts of it will cause your body to lose fluid and magnify the losses you'll incur while riding. This lowers performance. In fact, fluid replacement should be your primary refueling concern during a commute. Drinking about one bottle of water per hour should be sufficient unless it's extremely hot and humid.

Middle Distance

Intensity: moderate basic training ride
Distance: 15 to 50 miles
Time: 45 minutes to 3 hours

Nutritionally, there are two dangers to avoid on training rides. The first is allowing your glycogen stores to become depleted—also known as the bonk. This can happen on rides of 2 hours or more. The second is dehydration, a loss of body fluid that results in sluggishness.

You can avoid both conditions by using a sports drink. It will supply glucose and liquid simultaneously in a form that's quickly usable by the body. Resist the temptation to rely exclusively on these drinks, however. Dr. Applegate also recommends drinking water on long rides since sweat loss outweighs the need for energy replacement. Carry two bottles—one filled with a sports drink and the other with plain water. Alternately drink from each one every 10 to 20 minutes.

There are other key nutrition rules to remember. We mentioned these before, but let's go over them again. Never eat fatty foods prior to riding. Pastries, chocolate, and cream cheese take longer to digest and contain less readily available fuel. Instead, eat a high-carbohydrate meal or snack. Remember that carbohydrate should comprise 60 to 70 percent of your daily caloric intake, especially if you ride on consecutive days. Since individual needs are different, you may want to carry a high-carbo energy bar as well. For a 2-hour ride, between 100 and 200 calories should be enough.

About 20 minutes before a training ride you should also drink 8 to 20 ounces of water. This is particularly important during the summer when you sweat more.

Intervals

Intensity: variable speed, high-intensity efforts interspersed with active recovery
Distance: 10 to 30 miles
Time: 30 minutes to 2 hours

Interval training is the best way to become a faster cyclist. It's also a good way to sting your muscles with excess lactic acid. Intense exertion produces lactic acid within the muscles, which eventually inhibits their ability to contract. It has been theorized that certain foods, such as cranberries and prunes, work as a buffer against acid buildup and delay muscle fatigue, but there's still no evidence to support this. In fact, there's a much more important factor involved—blood. It's largely responsible for flushing away metabolites such as lactic acid during high-intensity workouts.

For this reason it's crucial your blood not be wasted in the digestive tract when you're doing intervals. To ensure this, you should allow 2 to 4 hours for digestion before an intense ride. You should also drink at least 16 ounces of water beforehand, since losses from perspiration will be great.

When on the bike, drink water between every interval. You don't need a sports drink or snack on this type of ride unless your ride will exceed 2 hours. If it will, fill one bottle with a sports drink.

Hills

Intensity: more than 50 percent of the route involves climbing
Distance: 10 to 30 miles

Time: 2½ hours or less

A hilly ride taps your carbohydrate reserves. So the key is to plan ahead and eat a meal of about 600 calories (e.g., yogurt, bagel, fruit, low-fat cookies) between 2 and 4 hours beforehand.

If you do this and still run low on fuel, experiment with foods and liquids that are high in sugar, such as soda, undiluted fruit juice, and cookies. Ingest them just 15 minutes or less before you get on the bike and the sugar will usually kick in when your legs begin to fade.

Preride nutrition is especially important for a hilly outing because eating on the bike is virtually impossible. However, you can get some energy replenishment in transit. Just fill a water bottle with a sports drink, and take swigs whenever you're descending or when the grade is moderate enough for you to control the bike with one hand next to the stem.

After the ride, be sure to refuel. This is essential to ensure proper recovery after such a hard effort. Be sure to eat enough carbohydrate and drink plenty of fluid, so your glycogen stores will be nearly back to normal in 24 hours. You can also use one of many commercial drinks called carbo-loaders that are specifically designed to help you refuel properly without spending all night at the dinner table.

Long Distance

Intensity: low to moderate, steady speed
Distance: 50 to 100 miles or more
Time: 4 hours plus

A century is one type of ride where you can't survive on bad nutrition. When a cyclist fails on a long ride, it's usually due to poor eating habits. The key is good planning before, during, and after the big event.

During a century you'll probably ride slower than normal, which means you'll burn more fat for energy. Nonetheless, carbohydrate stores are still the limiting factor. Make sure yours are high by eating lots of carbo-rich foods in the days preceding the event. Stay off the bike the final day or two before the ride, and your muscles will be packed with glycogen.

The day of the century, eat a big preride meal. A pancake breakfast (light on the butter and syrup, of course) with fruit and plenty of water should do the trick.

Plan carefully for how and what you'll eat during the ride. Most organized centuries feature food stops. If not, carry sandwiches made with moderately low-fat ingredients such as jam, honey, apple butter, and bananas, or other high-carbo snacks. Pack them in small plastic bags you can open with one hand. Keep them in your jersey pocket and nibble on them throughout the ride. Your body handles a steady intake of small food portions much better than one or two overloads.

Forget high-fat goodies such as candy bars. These provide more fat and less carbohydrate than you need, as well as few necessary vitamins and minerals. Caffeine, in the form of soda, may provide some energy (most likely due to its sugar content), but research shows that it has less effect if you're a daily caffeine user.

Of course, fluid replacement is crucial. Carry at least four water bottles if there are no water stops along the route. For carbo nourishment, you can rely on either solid foods or sports drinks.

Within 6 hours after your long ride, it's important that you replenish exhausted glycogen stores. If you plan to ride again the next day, start eating and drinking immediately to ensure proper refueling.

A century is a great achievement, and you may want to toast yourself with a glass of champagne at ride's end. But wait a few hours if you can. Alcohol can interfere with glycogen refueling and body fluid balance.

10 AVOIDING AN UPSET STOMACH

It can happen anytime—at the crest of a steep hill, during an impromptu training sprint, at the start of an important race, or during a long ride in hot weather. Suddenly, your stomach doesn't feel so good. Though the queasiness usually passes, it sometimes can leave you retching by the roadside.

Experts agree that exercise-induced nausea is most likely to occur among novice riders or those trying to get back in shape after a long layoff. Says James Stray-Gunderson, M.D., who works in the human performance lab at the University of Texas Southwestern, "It's a common thing and nothing to be concerned about.

The fitter you get, the less it tends to happen. However, even fit people, if they're really going for it, can become nauseated and throw up."

Scientists aren't sure of all the causes, but they list the following as the main culprits.

Slowed gastric emptying. Both exercise and digestion require increased blood flow. When you ride with a lot of food or fluid in your belly, the stomach and working muscles battle for extra blood. And "your muscles always win," as registered dietitian Evelyn Tribole, a spokesperson for the American Dietetic Association, puts it. The result is that food doesn't leave the stomach as quickly as it should, and nausea may occur.

According to George Brooks, Ph.D., a professor of exercise physiology at the University of California at Berkeley, it's when your intensity approaches 75 to 80 percent of your VO_2 max—your maximum aerobic ability—that blood is shunted away from the stomach. Since training improves oxygen uptake, Brooks explains that being fit "allows you to exercise harder and still move things through." He also suspects that gastric emptying may improve with training. In other words, the more you ride while eating and drinking, the more efficient your digestive system becomes.

Physical irritation of the stomach lining. Brian Maxwell, a former world-class marathoner and the co-originator of PowerBars, says that exercise-related nausea can be induced by liquid sloshing in the stomach for long periods, which irritates the mucous membrane. While road riders would be far less susceptible than runners (who do have a higher rate of nausea and vomiting), this could be an important factor for mountain bikers.

Maxwell explains that eliminating this possible cause was part of the rationale behind adding oat bran to PowerBars. Theoretically, soluble fiber absorbs water, expands to an easily digestible gel, then slowly releases water and nutrients into the bloodstream.

Lowered pH. According to Dr. Stray-Gunderson, vigorous riding exhausts the energy substrates—or fuel—in cells and produces acids. If the level of exercise is so high that the body is unable to buffer these acids, your pH level will fall, triggering nausea, headache, restlessness, and weakness.

Dehydration. This can compound the problem of lowered pH. If you are insufficiently hydrated to produce sweat for vital body cooling, the necessary fluid will be pulled from your blood. Thus, the pH effect worsens. As Dr. Stray-Gunderson explains, "You don't have enough blood to absorb and buffer the acids being produced."

But, as few riders seem to realize, dehydration alone can cause nausea. And the process is a vicious cycle. If you're riding in hot weather and don't drink enough, you'll become dehydrated and nauseated. And once your stomach is upset, you won't want to put anything in it (particularly warm water), so the problem is compounded.

Anxiety. Those prerace stomach butterflies can stress your system just as much as high-intensity exercise and heat. And according to registered dietitian Ellen Coleman, an exercise physiologist and marathon athlete, "Whenever you stress the gastrointestinal system, it slows down." Because digestion isn't a priority in an emergency (such as an impending race), the brain slows stomach contractions, which impedes digestion. It isn't surprising, then, that a nervous cyclist with food and fluid in his stomach might get nauseated.

There are other, more obvious causes of nausea, including excessive alcohol consumption the night before a long ride or a race, too much caffeine (especially if you aren't accustomed to it), rich foods, food poisoning, and even flu. If you find that nausea is a chronic problem when you ride, there may be something more serious at work, and you should consult a physician.

Simple Solutions

If you're a hard-charger, occasional nausea may be inevitable. Often, however, it can be avoided by following a few simple precautions.

1. Eat sensibly the night before you ride. Ingest bland, high-carbohydrate foods and little or no alcohol and caffeine.

2. Eat lightly before an event. Tribole recommends a small meal of 500 to 700 calories 3 hours before the start. This might consist of a bowl of oatmeal with nonfat milk, a banana, and a raisin English muffin. Or eat a 200-calorie snack, such as four graham crackers or a slice of bread and a glass of juice, 1 or 2 hours prior to the ride.

3. Before and during the ride, avoid foods high in fat and insoluble fiber. These are difficult to digest and stay in the stomach longer. Instead, eat foods that are easily digestible and high in complex carbohydrate such as bread, cereal, muffins, crackers, pretzels, and pasta.

4. Avoid highly acidic foods such as citrus fruits, which can exacerbate the problem of lowered pH. If you become nauseated after using citrus-flavored sports drinks, switch to other solutions.

5. If you're doing an especially long ride and you'll have to eat during it, practice doing so in training so your stomach gets used to absorbing things during exercise.

6. Use training sessions to test foods and fluids, and eliminate those that create problems. Don't experiment during an important event.

7. For efforts of 2 to 4 hours, sports drinks with a carbohydrate concentration of 5 to 8 percent are adequate. For ultra events, higher concentrations may be necessary. Select glucose polymer or maltodextrin beverages, which are more readily absorbed than simple sugar solutions.

8. Stay hydrated by drinking lots of water in the days preceding the event. If you're awake early enough on the day of the event, consume several glasses 3 hours before the race. Then, just 5 minutes prior to the start, drink another 10 to 15 ounces.

9. During the ride, don't wait until you're thirsty to drink. Instead, drink at preplanned intervals—be sure to take in at least 4 ounces of water every 15 minutes (in addition to your sports drink).

10. After the race, be sure to drink plenty of cool liquids. Stay away from alcoholic beverages for the time being since they act like a diuretic.

11. Cool water is more palatable and better absorbed. The night before, chill one of your water bottles and freeze the other for a steady source of refreshing fluids.

12. Clean your water bottles after each ride, particularly if you use sports drinks.

Part Three
EATING SMART

11 BUYER'S GUIDE TO SPORTS DRINKS AND FOODS

As you can verify anytime you take a long ride, after about 2 hours of cycling, the energy that has been stored in your muscles as glycogen is gone. Then you have two choices. You can refuel the muscles by ingesting more carbohydrate, or suffer the pain and possible humiliation of bonking. To avoid the latter, let's examine various sports drinks and foods on the market and which ones are best for your needs. Each one has been specially formulated to make it easy to keep your carbohydrate level high.

Sports Drinks

These are favored by many recreational riders and racers. Most are 5 to 10 percent carbohydrate solutions. Like water, they fight dehydration by replacing lost body fluid. But more important, they supply carbohydrate, which is essential for prolonged muscle performance.

A drink with this dilution reaches the bloodstream at about the same rate as water. This means that the carbohydrate undergoes minimal digestion and can be quickly converted into muscle energy.

Not all carbohydrate sources are created equal, though. Some work better and more quickly than others. The most common sources found in commercially prepared drinks are glucose, glucose polymers, sucrose, maltodextrin, and fructose.

Glucose and sucrose are simple sugars. Glucose polymer and maltodextrin are chains of glucose molecules. In the 1970s and early 1980s, some research showed that the last two sources emptied from the stomach quicker than simple sugars, but recent studies indicate no difference.

However, Christine Wells, Ph.D., an exercise physiologist and professor of health and physical education at Arizona State University, prefers drinks formulated with glucose polymers. She explains that even if the polymers empty from the stomach at the same rate as simple sugars, a chain of glucose molecules is capable of delivering more carbohydrate.

Drinks listing fructose as the main carbohydrate are another matter. Fructose is a simple sugar found in fruit. It's used primarily as a sweetener, but is the main carbohydrate source for drinks such as Gear Up and Flash. Some studies have shown that fructose is more likely than the other sugars to cause cramping and bloating in the stomach and intestines. Also, it may not be absorbed as quickly as the other carbo sources.

Sodium and other electrolytes, such as potassium and chloride, are added to drinks to help maintain fluid balances within the body. Perspiration contains trace amounts of electrolytes, mostly sodium, but you don't usually sweat out enough to lower the levels in your blood. In rare cases, marathon runners and long-distance cyclists who consumed large quantities of water or other sodium-free beverages have suffered "water intoxication." They lost too much sodium, resulting in diluted blood. Water intoxication, or hyponatremia, causes headaches, cramping, loss of strength, and nausea. Most nutritionists say a healthful diet will maintain normal sodium levels, but taking in extra electrolytes won't hurt. Ironically, active people on low-salt diets can benefit from the added sodium in some energy drinks because their diets alone won't replenish lost body salts.

Adding electrolytes is about the only thing the new low-calorie energy drinks do. Body Fuel 100, Workout Light, and Gatorade Light all contain low percentages of carbohydrate because they're made for people trying to lose weight. None of these drinks adds enough carbohydrate to significantly replenish glycogen stores, but they're useful if you want to drink something tastier than water.

Concentrated Carbo Drinks

Carbo-loaders and replenishers have a higher concentration of carbohydrate than sports drinks, usually around 20 percent.

Studies have shown that solutions over 11 percent don't empty as quickly from the stomach, slow fluid absorption, and possibly cause nausea and diarrhea if consumed during exercise. Of these products, only Ultra Energy is marketed as appropriate to use on the bike. You should experiment to see what concentration you can handle while riding. Others should be used before or after riding.

These high-calorie products are most popular among ultra-marathon cyclists, who use them as meal replacements. Because blood is diverted from the stomach to the working muscles during exercise, as discussed in earlier chapters, solids take longer to digest than liquids. That's why that pasta you usually eat before a race sometimes just sits in your stomach and causes distress. Even a highly concentrated liquid is better and easier on your stomach.

Most cyclists find these carbo drinks beneficial before or after a ride. They're good for those who don't like to train or race on a full stomach, but who need a carbo boost a couple of hours beforehand. They can also be used with meals to carbo-load in the days prior to an important ride. And they are helpful afterward to replenish glycogen stores and recover quickly.

Energy Foods

For riders who prefer something to bite on, an energy bar may be the answer. Because it takes longer to digest, solid food is usually best suited to slower riding, such as touring or centuries. But many pro teams consume large quantities of energy bars during races. Be careful, though. Some products, such as Hoffman's Energy Bars, are surprisingly high in fat—14 grams or 54 percent, which is more than a Milky Way.

Energy bars pack a lot of carbohydrate into a little space. For instance, PowerBar's 40 grams is almost double what you'd get from such handy on-bike foods as an apple or banana.

GoPower is food in a tube. It's not quite solid, although there are small chunks suspended in the dark liquid, but it's definitely not a drink. It's sweet, with a lingering aftertaste. GoPower uses no preservatives and gets its carbohydrate from cane juice, green walnuts, and lemon juice. One serving provides 110 percent of the U.S. RDA of vitamins C, B, thiamine, and riboflavin. The tube is handy and mess-free.

(continued on page 51)

TABLE 11–1.
Analysis of Sports Drinks and Foods Energy Drinks

Product/ Manufacturer	Size	Carbohydrate Source	Flavor	Avg. Cost ($)	Per 16-oz. Water Bottle			Claims
					Carbohydrate (%)	Calories	Sodium (mg)	
Body Fuel 750/ Vitex Foods, Inc.	1.25-lb. cannister, single-serve packets	maltodextrin, fructose	orange	1.36	7	140	140	Manufacturer advises either a 4% or 7% solution, according to preference.
Body Fuel 100/ Vitex Foods, Inc.	12 packets containing 0.3 gram each	maltodextrin, NutraSweet	lemon-lime	0.90	1	10	60	Strong NutraSweet aftertaste.
Breakthrough/ Weider Health & Fitness	16-oz. bottle or box of 8, 6-oz. packets	maltodextrin, fructose	lemon	1.20	8	320	56	Has trace of fat (less than 1 gram), but more than other drinks.

(continued)

TABLE 11–1.

Analysis of Sports Drinks and Foods—*Continued*

Energy Drinks—*continued*

Product/ Manufacturer	Size	Carbohydrate Source	Flavor	Avg. Cost ($)	Per 16-oz. Water Bottle			Claims
					Carbohydrate (%)	Calories	Sodium (mg)	
CarboGold/ NutriQuest, Inc.	1.1-lb. cannister	maltodextrin, fructose	citrus	0.70	6.9	80	10	Official drink of 7-Eleven cycling team.
Cytomax/ Champion Nutrition	1-lb. cannister w/bike bottle, 3-lb. cannister	Metacarb	apple	1.58	11	110	100	Metacarb is a blend of carbohydrate from Indian maize.
ERG/Gookinaid	packets and tub in pints, quarts, half-gallons, gallons and kilos	glucose	orange. lemon, fruit punch, competition	0.60	5.7	90	70	Manufacturer recommends not using the orange and fruit punch flavors during competition because of their strong aftertaste.

Product / Company	Form	Carbohydrate source	Flavors					Comments
Exceed Fluid Replacement and Energy Drink/Ross Labs	1.5-lb. cannister, bottle-size pouch, 1-qt. bottle	glucose polymer, fructose	orange, lemon-lime	0.80	7.2	140	50	The first drink to use glucose polymer.
Flash/Hoffman's	1.12-lb. cannister	fructose	orange	0.60	8	120	110	Tart orange flavor, little aftertaste.
Gatorade/Quaker Oats Co.	canned liquid, liquid concentrate, and bottled liquid in sizes from 8-oz. single servings to kilos	sucrose, glucose	lemon-lime, orange, fruit punch, lemon-ade	0.55	6	100	110	The original, developed in 1965 for the University of Florida football team—the Gators.
Gatorade Light/Quaker Oats Co.	16-oz. bottle	glucose	lemon-lime, orange, citrus cooler	0.80	2.6	100	80	Low in calories without artificial sweeteners.

(continued)

TABLE 11-1.
Analysis of Sports Drinks and Foods—*Continued*
Energy Drinks—*continued*

Product/Manufacturer	Size	Carbohydrate Source	Flavor	Per 16-oz. Water Bottle				Claims
				Avg. Cost ($)	Carbohydrate (%)	Calories	Sodium (mg)	
Gear Up/R. J. Corr Naturals	10- and 32-oz. bottle	fructose	fruit punch, orange	0.45	13	240	less than 5	It's the official drink of the Chicago Bears, and contains fruit pulp.
Glucolyte/Nutri-Power	16-oz. cannister	maltodextrin, fructose	orange	0.50	7	120	30	Has a slight milky smell and taste—like a creamsicle.
Second Wind/Pro-Line	35.2-oz. cannister, 16-oz. packet	maltodextrin, fructose	light, sweet, milky flavor	1.70	8	100	70	Contains nonfat dry milk. Manufacturer suggests mixing with fruit juice or milk and using as a dietary supplement.

				Avg. Cost ($)	Carbohydrate (%)	Calories	Sodium (mg)	Claims
Snap-Up/Snapple Natural Beverage Co.	16-oz. bottle	maltodextrin, fructose	lemon, orange	0.70	8	160	58	Both flavors are light and leave no aftertaste.
Workout/White Rock Products	16-oz. bottle, 1-lb. cannister	glucose polymer, glucose	lemon-lime, lemonade, orange, punch	0.50	8	160	30	Developed by Ed Burke, Ph.D., former director of sports science and technology for the U.S. cycling team.
Workout Light/White Rock Products	16-oz. bottle	glucose polymer, NutraSweet	iced tea	0.70	2.5	50	19	Formulated for the calorie conscious. Has added calcium.

Concentrated Carbo Drinks

Product/Manufacturer	Size	Carbohydrate Source	Flavor	Avg. Cost ($)	Per 16-oz. Carbohydrate (%)	Per 16-oz. Calories	Per 16-oz. Sodium (mg)	Claims
Carboloader/Nutri-Power	12-oz. cannister	maltodextrin	citrus	1.00	13	220	0	Manufacturer suggests using as a dietary supplement.

(continued)

TABLE 11-1.

Analysis of Sports Drinks and Foods—*Continued*
Concentrated Carbo Drinks—*continued*

Product/ Manufacturer	Size	Carbohydrate Source	Flavor	Avg. Cost ($)	Carbohydrate (%)	Calories	Sodium (mg)	Claims
						Per 16-oz.		
Exceed High Carbohydrate Source/Ross Labs	2-qt. packet	glucose polymer, sucrose	golden punch, citrus punch	2.20	23	470	234	1 packet gives the carbohydrate equivalent of 11 medium-size baked potatoes.
Gatorlode/Quaker Oats Co.	19-oz. cannister	maltodextrin, dextrose	citrus, banana, lemon	1.80	20	374	126	Manufacturer recommends drinking 2, 12-oz. servings per day for 3 or 4 days before competition.
Payload/Hoffman's	28-oz. cannister	maltodextrin, fructose	orange	1.50	21	400	220	No aftertaste.

| Ultra Energy/Procyon | 4-oz. packet | maltodextrin, dextrose, sucrose, lactose (in chocolate) | chocolate, grape | 7.00 | 23 | 360 | 126 | The favored drink of some RAAM riders. |
| Ultra Fuel/Twin Lab | 16-oz. bottle | glucose polymer, crystalline, fructose | fruit punch, lemon-lime | 1.80 | 23 | 400 | 0 | No sodium, and added B complex vitamins. |

Energy Foods

Product/Manufacturer	Size (oz.)	Carbohydrate Source	Flavor	Avg. Cost ($)	Carbohydrate (%)	Calories	Fat (mg)	Claims
Energize/Nutri-Power	1.50	glucose, fructose		0.99	76	144	0	Nutty taste, contains no dyes or preservatives. Does contain bee pollen.
Energy Bars/Hoffman's	1.75	glucose	molasses	0.69	55	232	14	High fat content and the chocolate coatings melt easily.
	1.75	sucrose	peanut butter	0.69	53	258	14	
	2.00	sucrose	club	0.69	60	296	16	

(continued)

TABLE 11-1.
Analysis of Sports Drinks and Foods—*Continued*
Energy Foods—*continued*

Product/ Manufacturer	Size	Carbohydrate Source	Flavor	Avg. Cost ($)	Carbohydrate (%)	Calories	Sodium (mg)	Claims
finHälsa	1.70	glucose		0.50	56	170	2	Official supplier of the 7-Eleven cycling team.
Meal on the Go/ Provesta Corp.	1.50	fructose	original, apple	0.50	59	145	4	Fruity taste, firm texture, not overly dry.
PowerBar/Power-food, Inc.	2.25	fructose	choco-late, wild berry, malt	1.50	61	225	2	Manufacturer advises eating 1 bar every hour during exercise with 8-16 ounces of water.
GoPower/Kario	0.35	sucrose, fructose		0.40	66	27	0.01	The semi-liquid is concentrated and can be eaten straight from the tube.

Choosing
the Right Energy Source

Read labels carefully and experiment with different brands until you find one you like. Don't underestimate the role of taste. If you don't like a drink or bar, you won't consume enough of it to reap the benefits. Do your testing on the bike, too. Research by Quaker Oats shows that your sense of taste changes during exercise. The drinks have been designed with that in mind. What seems overly sweet in the kitchen may be just right on the road, or vice versa.

Keep the drinks cool, too. Temperature not only plays a role in taste but also effectiveness. A cool beverage is refreshing, and studies have shown that cold liquids lower core body temperature. Plus, it's digested and gets to work faster than a warm solution.

Source List for Energy Foods

To obtain more information about specific products or find a nearby dealer, write to these addresses.

- Body Fuel 100/750: Vitex Foods, Inc., 1821 E. 48th Pl., Los Angeles, CA 90058
- Breakthrough: Weider Health & Fitness, 211100 Erwin St., Woodland Hills, CA 91367
- CarboGold: NutriQuest, Inc., 2132 Richards St., Douglas, WY 82633
- Cytomax: Champion Nutrition, 2615 Stanwell Dr., Concord, CA 94520
- ERG: Gookinaid, 4475 University Ave., San Diego, CA 92105
- Exceed: Ross Labs, 625 Cleveland Ave., Columbus, OH 43215
- finHälsa: Inertia Inc., 8055 Manchester Ave., Suite 550, Playa del Rey, CA 90293
- Flash, Payload, Energy Bars (Hoffman's Food Products): Distributed by York Barbell Co., Inc., Box 1707, Dept. M, York, PA 17405
- Gatorade, Gatorade Light, Gatorlode: Quaker Oats Co., Merchandise Mart, Chicago, IL 60654.

- Gear Up: R. J. Corr Naturals, Box 10437, Chicago, IL 60610
- Glucolyte, Carboloader, Energize: Nutri-Power, Box 1312, Northbrook, IL 60062
- GoPower: Kario, 2540 Main St., Suite U200, Irvine, CA 92714
- Meal on the Go: Provesta Corp., 15 Phillips Bldg., Bartlesville, OK 74004
- PowerBar: Powerfood, Inc., 2448 6th St., Berkeley, CA 94702
- Second Wind: Pro-Line Nutritional Products, Inc., 1731 W. Rose Garden Ln. No. 1, Phoenix, AZ 85027
- Snap-Up: Snapple Natural Beverage Co., 1535 Schaefer St., Ridgewood, NY 11385
- Ultra Energy: Procyon, 13306 E. Whittier Blvd., Whittier, CA 90606
- Ultra Fuel: Twin Lab, 2120 Smithtown Ave., Ronkonkoma, NY 11779
- Workout, Workout Light: White Rock Products, 16-16 Whitestone Expressway, Whitestone, NY 11357

ALTERNATIVES TO PASTA

It's the night before a century and everybody's gobbling pasta. Normally you'd be doing the same. After all, you know the importance of consuming high-carbohydrate foods before a long ride. But as you lift your spaghetti-laden fork, something inside you snaps. You can't do it. Linguine, ziti, manicotti, fettuccine—you've had all you can stand. Isn't there another way to get the needed fuel?

Fortunately, the Italians don't have a monopoly on carbohydrate. Many other foods work just as well as pasta. Oriental, Eastern, Mexican, and some American fare can offer your taste buds variation while giving the rest of your body what it needs for endurance.

Even a normal American diet (46 percent carbohydrate) will enable you to exercise hard (75 percent of your VO_2 max) for about 2 hours before experiencing glycogen depletion. However, after a good carbohydrate loading you can exert yourself for 3 hours or more.

The other fuel sources, namely fat and protein, don't work

nearly as well. Fat interferes with the building of glycogen stores. While protein helps build muscle tissue, most diets provide more than you need, and part of the excess is turned into body fat.

Generally, your diet should be 60 to 70 percent carbohydrate, 20 to 30 percent fat, and 10 to 15 percent protein. However, in the days before an important long ride, you should increase carbohydrate intake while decreasing fat and protein. Here's how to do it without setting foot in an Italian restaurant.

Oriental

The major ingredients in Oriental food—rice, noodles, and vegetables—are rich in carbohydrate. Small amounts of meat or fish are also used. This combination offers the necessary proportion of carbohydrate to protein and fat.

Keep in mind that how the food is prepared is almost as important as the ingredients. When ordering Oriental fare, choose dishes that are stir-fried to avoid excess fat. Don't order spare ribs or deep-fried items. These provide more fat and protein than you need.

Eastern

Eastern foods such as those from Thailand, Korea, Vietnam, and India feature beans, rice, grains, vegetables, and breads, all of which are high in carbohydrate and low in fat. In addition, Eastern food is often steamed, thus adding little fat. While it might not be easy to find a good Eastern restaurant, it's worth looking for. On the night before a big ride, this may be the perfect pasta alternative.

Mexican

Mexican food is a widely available alternative to pasta. However, be careful to order the right items. Tortillas, beans, and rice are good because they are high in carbohydrate and low in fat. Fried rice and refried beans are also carbo-rich, but the frying adds unwanted evils. For example, beans normally have little or no fat, but refried beans are 30 percent fat. This won't help you build glycogen and neither will Mexican dishes containing too much meat or cheese. Avoid enchiladas and tacos.

How to Carbo-Load

The most effective way to carbo-load is as follows: Six days before your big event, ride hard for 90 minutes. On this day your intake should be about 50 percent carbohydrate. Continue this diet for two days, but decrease your training to about 40 minutes per day to preserve glycogen stores. The next two days reduce your training to about 20 minutes each and consume 70 percent carbohydrate. To achieve this percentage, eat no more calories than normal but increase your intake of bread, fruit, vegetables, and other high-carbohydrate foods while avoiding fried and fatty ones. Rest the day before the ride and continue your high-carbohydrate diet. This will leave your glycogen stores brimming for the big ride.

Note that carbo-loading works only if you've been training. Regular activity increases your capacity for glycogen storage. If you're unfit, your muscles won't store more than their usual amount of glycogen, and any extra carbohydrate calories will be converted to fat.

Even if you're well trained, carbo-loading can have negative side effects. High levels of glycogen cause fluid retention, which creates moderate weight gain and may make your legs feel stiff and heavy. But once you start lowering your glycogen levels by cycling, the discomfort will disappear.

After you complete the big ride, rebuild your energy stores with another high-carbohydrate meal. The postride foods preferred by most cyclists include fruit, breads, pizza, and the ever-present pasta. But who knows? Maybe chicken lo mein will soon find its way onto the list.

13 JUNK FOOD, FAST FOOD

Nutritionists write books on the subject. Researchers conduct long, extensive studies. Magazines publish monthly columns. But in the end, sports nutrition often comes down to pacing the aisles of a 7-Eleven or perusing the menu board at McDonald's when you're halfway through a ride and hungry. If you can make the right choices in these situations, you may know all that's necessary about cycling nutrition.

The first thing to realize is the value of carbohydrate. As explained in previous chapters, this is your body's most effective fuel for exercise. Foods that offer a high percentage of carbohydrate are digested faster and used more efficiently than foods that are high in fat or protein. The ideal cycling food should be at least 55 percent carbohydrate and no more than 30 percent fat. With all of this in mind, let's take a stroll through a convenience store to evaluate some typical choices. Afterward, we'll stop at a fast-food restaurant to learn the best (and worst) selections there.

Making the Right Choices at the Convenience Store

Snack items. A 2-ounce bag of potato chips offers 306 calories, but 58 percent come from fat. By comparison, a bag of tortilla chips has about the same number of total calories, but only 42 percent are from fat—better than potato chips but still not low enough.

Nuts and seeds are even worse. Split a 6-ounce can of peanuts with your riding partner and you'll each get 471 calories. A whopping 77 percent of these are fat calories, while only 13 percent are carbohydrate. Likewise, half a can of almonds translates into 270 calories, of which 80 percent are fat and 13 percent are carbohydrate. And of the 314 calories in a 2-ounce pouch of sunflower seeds, 76 percent are fat and 14 percent are carbohydrate.

So in this aisle, the best choice is a bag of pretzels (salt-free, if possible). Unlike nuts and seeds, they aren't naturally high in fat. And unlike chips, they aren't fried. If you eat half of a 10-ounce bag of pretzel sticks, you'll get 550 calories, of which 81 percent are carbohydrate and only 6 percent are fat.

Cookies. On a long ride you can easily burn 3,000 to 5,000 calories. Thus, you need high-calorie replenishment. Cookies provide plenty of calories, but they're often the wrong kind. For instance, two chocolate chip cookies supply about 102 calories. But 41 percent of these are from fat. Two oatmeal cookies give about 118 calories, of which 38 percent are fat.

Fig bars are the wisest selection in this aisle. Two give you 106 calories—83 percent from carbohydrate and just 17 percent from fat. Since their calorie content is about a third lower than that of most cookies, you can have three times as many. This helps satisfy your appetite.

Candy bars. As part of an everyday diet, candy bars and other junk foods are a bad idea. Besides being fattening, they offer few nutrients.

However, during a ride, sugary foods can play an important role by providing a quick shot of carbohydrate. The trick is to get this boost without also getting a large dose of fat. This isn't easy. A Snickers bar (270 calories) contains about an equal proportion of fat and carbohydrate. The same can be said for most candy bars, except 3 Musketeers and Milky Way. Of the latter's 260 calories, 66 percent come from carbohydrate and 31 percent come from fat.

Pastries. Because of their creams and fillings, most pastry items provide more fat than carbohydrate. For instance, a Hostess cake doughnut (115 calories) is 55 percent fat.

Believe it or not, the best choice in this category may be that old junk food standard, Twinkies. That's right, two of them provide 286 calories—68 percent from carbohydrate and only 26 percent from fat.

Ice cream and yogurt. While regular ice cream is extremely high in fat, some related products make pretty good cycling fuel. Of the 167 calories in an ice-cream sandwich, for instance, nearly two-thirds come from carbohydrate and only a third from fat. A Popsicle's even better. All of its 65 calories come from sugar, which is a form of carbohydrate.

But the best selection in the dairy case is yogurt. A cup of fruit-flavored, low-fat yogurt (225 calories) is 75 percent carbohydrate and only 10 percent fat. And unlike ice-cream sandwiches and Popsicles, yogurt is nutritious, providing more calcium and B vitamins.

Cold drinks. It's easy to find high-carbohydrate sources in this area. Twelve ounces of soda supply 140 to 180 calories, all of which are carbohydrate from sugar. A more nutritious alternative that's also 100 percent carbohydrate is fruit juice (180 calories per 12 ounces). But the best choice is Gatorade. Besides being totally carbohydrate, it replaces potassium and other elements lost in sweat, and it is designed to reach your bloodstream quickly.

Fruit. If you find a convenience store or corner market with fresh fruit, go for it. Fruit is nearly 100 percent carbohydrate and a good provider of vitamins, minerals, and fiber. A banana has 105 calories, an apple about 80, and an orange about 60. For endurance and nutrition, this is your best option.

The Best of Fast Food

Most cyclists know that fast food is generally high in fat and low in nutrients. However, a fast-food restaurant is often the most convenient place to get a meal during a ride. So is it possible to refuel properly under the golden arches or at the home of the Whopper?

The answer is yes. One way is by avoiding the big-name burger. A McDonald's Big Mac, for instance, packs 563 calories—53 percent from fat and only 28 percent from carbohydrate. In addition, avoid french fries. A regular order adds 220 calories, of which half are fat. A chocolate shake isn't as bad (383 calories, 21 percent fat). But a burger, fries, and shake total 1,150 calories—a meal that's almost half fat.

A better option is a chicken sandwich with barbecue sauce, 6 ounces of orange juice, and a carton of low-fat milk. This gives you about 625 calories—more than half from carbohydrate and only 25 percent from fat.

The best types of fast food can be found at pizza or Mexican outlets. Four slices of a 12-inch cheese pizza (653 calories) are 59 percent carbohydrate and just 17 percent fat. Likewise, at Taco Bell, a bean tostada (179 calories), an order of beans and cheese (232 calories), or a bean burrito (350 calories) are each more than 50 percent carbohydrate and less than 30 percent fat—not quite as good as Twinkies, but a fine midride meal nonetheless.

14 MAKE ENERGY-PACKED MEALS WITH YOUR MICROWAVE

What to do after a day of working and cycling when you're too tired to cook, but you know you shouldn't fill up on fast food? If you're like most busy people, you pop a frozen dinner in the microwave. Done right, the entire process of cooking, eating, and cleaning up takes 15 minutes.

Although frozen fare is still imperfect in taste and nutrition, microwavable meals have improved a lot in recent years. If you choose brands carefully and eat wisely at other meals, they can have a legitimate place in an active lifestyle.

Shopping for the Best Entrée

While old-style TV dinners and the regular-line entrées from such companies as Stouffer's and Le Menu are high in fat (more than 50 percent in some cases), many of the new offerings are well below the recommended 30 percent level. Light & Elegant, Pritikin Quick Cuisine, Benihana, Chun King, and the Healthy Choice lines contain, on average, less than 20 percent fat.

When selecting a low-fat dinner, don't rely on words such as "lite" and "lean." Instead, study the fine print. A typical 300-calorie meal should contain no more than 10 grams of fat, which means it accounts for less than 30 percent of the total calories. (To calculate the percentage of fat calories for any dinner, multiply the number of grams of fat by nine and divide by total calories.)

The Pitfalls of Frozen Meals

While manufacturers are trimming fat, they're still pouring on the salt. Typically, sodium levels range from 600 to 1,200 milligrams, with some dinners as high as 2,000 milligrams. Ironically, many of the ultra-low-fat Oriental dishes are highest in sodium, an attempt no doubt to build the flavor lost with the fat. The best bets are the Healthy Choice, Pritikin, and Legume lines, which average around 500 milligrams.

Much of the sodium in some frozen dinners comes from the flavor-enhancer MSG. If you're sensitive to it, as many people are, look for it in the ingredients. It may be listed as monosodium glutamate or hydrolyzed vegetable protein.

Sulfites are another potentially dangerous food additive. In fact, they can cause severe, even fatal reactions in some people. Although they've been banned from fresh food, they may still appear as preservatives in some frozen potato and seafood dishes.

Another pitfall of frozen fare is that most meals are too meager to satisfy the legendary cyclist appetite. What's more, they generally don't supply enough essential vitamins and minerals.

(Most dinners provide less than 20 percent of the calcium, iron, and vitamins A, B, and C you need each day. Fiber is in short supply, too.)

How to Supplement a Microwave Meal

To avoid snacking later in the evening, supplement frozen dinners with low-fat dairy products, whole grain breads, and fresh fruits and vegetables. For example, you can greatly enhance the nutritional value of a frozen meal (and make it much more filling), by adding a salad with reduced-calorie dressing, a slice of whole wheat bread, a glass of nonfat milk, and a piece of fresh fruit. You'll get fewer than 300 additional calories and almost no added fat. Likewise, if you regularly eat frozen dinners, balance them with more nutritious breakfasts and lunches.

Despite all that can be done to make frozen meals more nutritious, there isn't much you can do to change their taste and texture. If you sampled everything in the market, chances are good that you wouldn't look forward to eating many of them again. You can make them slightly more palatable by adding judicious amounts of Mrs. Dash, Tabasco, lemon juice, or diced tomatoes and onions.

Create Your Own Entrée in Minutes

The best way to use a microwave is to create the meals yourself. And this needn't take a lot of time. For instance, prepare a large batch of a favorite food on your day off, then freeze individual portions in plastic containers for later use.

You can also cook quick dishes from scratch. It can be as simple as zapping a baked potato or steaming delicious al dente vegetables in paper towels, or you can create a mouth-watering dish such as teriyaki chicken in less than 10 minutes. Simply place skinned chicken breasts in a microwave-safe casserole dish and baste with bottled teriyaki sauce or a mixture of 1 tablespoon soy sauce, 2 tablespoons ketchup, and 2 teaspoons brown sugar. Cover tightly and microwave on high for 4 minutes. Baste again and zap an additional 2 to 3 minutes. Uncover and let stand for 5 minutes.

For the cost of a couple bland frozen dinners, you can also buy a microwave cookbook. Once you discover how easy, inexpensive, and appealing your own microwave meals are, frozen dinners may leave you cold.

TABLE 14–1.
Shopper's Guide

Product	Serving Size	Calories	Fat (%)	Sodium (mg)
Less than 30% fat				
Armour Dinner Classics Lite	11.0 oz.	260	23	871
Benihana Classic Dinners	11.0 oz.	319	20	1,321
Chun King Entrees	10.0 oz.	290	20	1,250
Healthy Choice	11.2 oz.	270	14	432
Le Menu Light Style Dinners	12.0 oz.	262	25	680
Light & Elegant	9.0 oz.	264	18	859
Mrs. Paul's Light Seafood	10.0 oz.	259	26	796
Pritikin Quick Cuisine	11.5 oz.	293	11	300
Stouffer's Lean Cuisine	10.0 oz.	261	28	934
31% to 40% fat				
Armour Dinner Classics	12.0 oz.	355	38	1,213
Banquet Family Entrees	8.0 oz.	229	39	983
Budget Gourmet	10.0 oz.	386	38	881
Budget Gourmet Slim Selects	10.0 oz.	283	32	831
Budget Gourmet 3-Dish	12.0 oz.	351	37	846
Celentano	10.0 oz.	327	40	484
Green Giant	10.0 oz.	334	31	1,104

NOTE: Numbers represent averages from product lines.

15 THE NEWS ON BOOZE

One year there was a competitor in the Ironman triathlon who rode the cycling leg with a six-pack of beer in his handlebar bag. He claimed drinking aided his performance. By the end of the 112-mile ride, he had downed all six cans.

Product	Serving Size	Calories	Fat (%)	Sodium (mg)
Legume Light Tofu Entrees	10.0 oz.	264	35	354
Le Menu L'Orient Dinners	11.0 oz.	388	34	945
Old El Paso Mexican Dinners	13.0 oz.	493	32	1,158
Patio Mexican Dinners	12.0 oz.	545	38	—
Stouffer's Dinner Supreme	12.0 oz.	370	37	1,013
Swanson 4-Part Dinners	12.0 oz.	450	39	977
Swanson Hungry Man Entrees	12.0 oz.	520	40	1,398
Weight Watchers	9.0 oz.	271	38	893
More than 41% fat				
Banquet Dinners	16.0 oz.	719	50	1,243
Barber Foods	7.0 oz.	426	47	957
Le Menu Dinners	11.0 oz.	401	42	985
Le Menu Entrees	8.0 oz.	355	51	783
Stouffer's Entrees	10.0 oz.	356	48	1,068
Swanson Entrees	9.0 oz.	350	54	833
Swanson Hungry Man Dinners	17.0 oz.	705	43	1,639
Swift International Entrees	6.0 oz.	358	42	865

SOURCE: Reprinted from "Nutrition Action Healthletter." Copyright ©1989, Center for Science in the Public Interest.

If you're like most cyclists, alcohol's role in your riding is probably not quite this overt. You may have a glass of beer or wine with lunch during a long ride. And during the evenings of a tour, you and your partners might raise a toast or two (or three) to your accomplishments. While it's not the same as sipping beer in the saddle, this type of drinking does have a surprisingly large influence on performance.

Alcohol Slows You Down

When you drink too much, you begin the following day's ride at a disadvantage. In addition to traditional hangover effects like headache and nausea, you'll probably be dehydrated.

Though it seems contradictory, drinking alcohol actually lowers your fluid levels. In fact, to metabolize a single ounce of alcohol, your body uses 8 ounces of water. Alcohol, like caffeine, is also a diuretic, which causes increased urination and water loss. Therefore, it's important to replenish any fluid losses before riding. Have one glass of water for every two drinks. (A drink is equal to a 12-ounce beer, a 4-ounce glass of wine, or 1½ ounces of 80-proof liquor. Each of these provides ½ ounce of pure alcohol.)

Even so, don't expect to be at your best. A U.S. Navy study found that it takes 36 hours for your body to fully recover from drunkenness. Interestingly, cycling or other aerobic exercise can speed the recovery by raising your body temperature, thus eliminating the alcohol more quickly.

Nonetheless, too much drinking is still detrimental to performance and your well-being. On long rides in cold weather, having alcohol in your blood may contribute to hypothermia (dangerously low body temperature). In warm weather, the risk of dehydration, heat exhaustion, and heatstroke increases with the amount of alcohol consumed.

In addition, half of all traffic deaths and a third of all traffic injuries are alcohol related. It's also a significant factor in home, industrial, and recreational mishaps. And long-term, excessive alcohol use leads to myriad serious health problems, including liver damage, high blood pressure, and abnormalities of the heart, brain, muscles, and esophagus.

Despite these dangers, moderate drinking has recently been touted as an effective protector against heart disease because it has been shown to increase the level of HDL (good) cholesterol in the blood. But according to one study, this effect occurs only in sedentary people. As a cyclist, your HDL level is probably already high and your heart is reaping its protective benefits. For you, moderate drinking would provide no added advantage. Similarly, in terms of cycling performance, modest drinking the night before doesn't help. However, unlike excessive drinking, it doesn't hurt either.

Determining the difference between moderate and excessive

alcohol intake isn't easy. Some experts believe the threshold between harmless and harmful is three drinks. Some claim it's okay
to have one drink for each 50 pounds of body weight. Others
insist alcohol tolerance depends on the individual.

In any case, you can probably sense when you're reaching
your threshold. If you want to ride at 100 percent the following
day, it's a good idea to heed your limit.

How Alcohol Travels through Your Body

To better explain, let's see what happens to alcohol in your
system. As you drink, it's absorbed directly from your stomach
and small intestine into the bloodstream. This process takes less
than an hour. Your body reacts by immediately trying to eliminate
the invading alcohol. The liver releases enzymes that begin this
breakdown. But your body can only get rid of about ¾ ounce of
alcohol per hour (the equivalent of 1½ beers, glasses of wine, or
mixed drinks).

Unlike caffeine or other performance enhancers, drinking
before or during a ride won't give you an energy boost. Since
your liver is busy processing alcohol, it decreases its output of
glucose, thus limiting this important muscle fuel and causing
premature fatigue during exercise. Meanwhile, the alcohol that's
waiting to be processed by the liver is unable to provide any
energy for the muscles. Even if it were available, alcohol is a weak
energy source because it doesn't contribute to the formation of
muscle glycogen, the body's preferred fuel for cycling.

These effects, in addition to dehydration, increase with the
amount of alcohol consumed. Naturally, a glass of beer or wine
with lunch won't noticeably inhibit your performance, but a few
glasses will.

Beer Is a Poor Carbo-Loader

Despite the belief of some riders, drinking beer is a poor
form of carbo-loading. A 12-ounce beer provides a scant 50 calories of carbohydrate. This isn't much compared to the effect it

has on your central nervous system. For instance, if you weigh 150 pounds, drinking five beers will raise your blood alcohol level to about 0.10, which makes you legally drunk in most states. At the same time, five beers provide only enough carbohydrate to ride about 10 miles.

Wine is an even worse choice for carbo-loading. A 4-ounce glass contains just 15 carbohydrate calories. The poorest carbo-loader, however, is liquor, which has no carbohydrate at all.

Alcoholic beverages contain mostly empty calories. Beer and wine do provide traces of protein, as well as some vitamins and minerals, but these nutrients are much more abundant in other drinks and foods.

Twelve ounces of regular beer contain about 150 calories. Light beer is, as the commercials say, less filling, but still provides a hefty 100 calories. A glass of wine or 1½ ounces of liquor also provide about 100 calories. If you're watching your weight, alcohol intake is a good place to look.

Of course, if you had talked with that guzzling competitor in the Ironman, he would have scoffed at the mention of excess weight. He would probably have claimed that beer helps him get through difficult races by lowering his inhibitions, nervousness, and feelings of fatigue.

However, what he may not have realized is that his "sports drink" is a depressant that disturbs motor skills, including the balance and coordination that's essential for proper bike handling. He probably wouldn't have known that it also causes premature exhaustion.

He could have been told all this. But at the finish, where the athletes gather, he was nowhere to be found.

Part Four

WHAT'S IN
THERE?

☐16 ARE SPORTS DRINKS AND FOODS HEALTHFUL?

Sports drinks and energy bars promise performance—and there's no question they deliver. Dozens of scientific studies have shown that by getting fuel to muscles quickly, these products extend endurance. Their popularity among cyclists is equally unquestionable.

But what is worth asking about is the health effects of these performance enhancers. With ominous sounding ingredients such as pyridoxine hydrochloride and nicotinamide, it's reasonable to wonder whether regular consumption can cause any long-term damage. In other words, sports drinks and energy bars are good for performance, but are they good for you?

To find out, in this chapter we'll evaluate the ingredients commonly found in these products. Each ingredient is usually one of three major food compounds (carbohydrate, fat, protein) or an additive. The additives serve a variety of functions—from enhancing flavor or color, to extending shelf life, to increasing nutrition. For instance, those unpronounceable "villains"—pyridoxine hydrochloride and nicotinamide—appear in sports drinks for nutritional value, providing vitamin B. They are simply the chemical names for the vitamin as it's found in plants or elsewhere in nature.

But all the ingredients may not be so benign. What follows is an explanation of those commonly found in energy products.

For each, we'll tell you why it's included and, more important, its effect on your health.

Carbohydrate

By law, labels must list ingredients according to the quantity in which they appear. This is why the first item you'll see on an energy product label is always some form of carbohydrate. It's your body's most effective fuel source during exercise and the main component of sports drinks and energy bars.

Carbohydrate comes in many forms. When you see malto-dextrin listed on a PowerBar wrapper, or corn syrup solids as the top ingredient on a can of Exceed, you're looking at a carbohydrate source. In both of these examples, it's a type of carbohydrate known as a glucose polymer. This is a short chain of molecules derived from complex carbohydrate. A glucose polymer provides a steadier release of energy than simple carbohydrate (sugar). And unlike complex carbohydrate (pasta, grains, potatoes, corn), it delivers the energy quickly. This is why maltodextrin and other glucose polymers are often used in energy products.

However, glucose polymers can be found in other foods, too. For instance, Jell-O pudding, Swiss Miss cocoa mix, and Teddy Graham snacks all contain maltodextrin. It adds texture, volume, and in some cases, flavor.

The Food and Drug Administration (FDA), which oversees food safety in the United States, has approved maltodextrin, put-ting it in the category of "generally recognized as safe," or GRAS. But this classification doesn't always mean an ingredient is harm-less. For example, sodium and potassium nitrites have been linked to cancer, but they still have GRAS status and are used on cured meats. The reason is that their benefits outweigh their hazards. (The nitrites help to prevent botulism, and a suitable substitute has yet to be developed.)

In addition to glucose polymers, energy products use other carbohydrate sources. Glucose (dextrose) and sucrose are chem-ical names for natural sugars that can deliver quick energy to the muscles. These ingredients are being used less frequently in sports drinks and bars because they can cause an insulin surge that has negative physical and mental effects. They also slow the absorption of water, which can cause hydration problems during exercise.

Another common sugar, fructose, is a natural component of everyday foods such as fruit and honey. All these are "generally recognized as safe" by the FDA.

Lactates are another class of ingredients considered safe. Some examples are alpha-polylactate and F-PolyaminoLactate. When you see the suffix "lactate" on a label, it means fructose and amino acids have been combined with lactate, a substance that provides energy without the debilitating effects associated with lactic acid. The result is an ingredient that doesn't disturb insulin levels. It does provide rapid energy and help neutralize the unwanted acid changes that occur in the blood during exercise.

Fat

As an exercise fuel, fat isn't as effective as carbohydrate during intense workouts. For this reason, most sports drinks contain no fat. This is good news, since a high-fat diet has been linked with heart disease and some forms of cancer. Nutritionists recommend that your diet be less than 35 percent fat.

The only sports drinks that contain fat are the small class of products intended as meal replacements. These drinks, such as Ultra Energy and ProOptibol, are used by many ultra-endurance cyclists who spend all day in the saddle. Fat appears on these labels under the guise of medium chain triglycerides. But the percentages are low enough to be harmless.

Energy bars, however, are a different story. Almost all contain fat, often in doses higher than recommended. On the label, look for ingredients such as sesame butter, peanut butter, peanuts, and vegetable oil. These are fat sources. Occasionally eating a fatty bar won't make you a candidate for a triple bypass, but if you down one several times a week, you are increasing your chances of having a high-fat diet. The Fast Break energy bar is 34 percent fat; Tiger's Milk Bar, 30 to 35 percent; and Hoffman's Energy Bar, 54 percent. By comparison, a Milky Way candy bar is 31 percent fat.

Not all energy bars are full of fat, however. The finHälsa is only 11 percent fat, while the PowerBar is just 8 percent. Interestingly, these bars consist mostly of ordinary ingredients. Their labels list raisins, wheat germ nuggets, brown rice, and peanut butter—a wholesome mix of high-carbohydrate ingredients with only a trace of fat.

Protein

Of the three main food compounds, protein is the least important energy source. It's instrumental in the building and repair of muscles but ineffective at providing them with fuel. That's why it's not included in most sports drinks but, like fat, is in meal replacement drinks and energy bars. Unlike fat, protein carries little health risk.

To find a protein source on the label of an energy bar or meal replacement drink, look for the words casein or albumin. The former is the principal protein of cow's milk, and the latter is a protein derived from egg whites. These harmless ingredients also appear in cottage cheese, yogurt, pancake mix, and ice cream.

Amino acids are another type of protein used in some meal replacement drinks, notably Ultra Energy. There are more than 20 amino acids that act as the building blocks of protein. Studies show that two of them, L-leucine and L-valine, may be beneficial during endurance exercise. (The "L" indicates it's in a biologically acceptable form.) Other popular amino acids include L-lysine, L-arginine, and L-tryptophan.

Because of the expense of isolating amino acids, they're not added to most bars or drinks. Rather, they're available as nutritional supplements. But since the majority of Americans get all the protein and amino acids they need from a routine diet, most nutritionists say such supplements are unnecessary.

Preservatives

Every processed food requires preservatives to keep it in its intended form. The most widely used is citric acid, which is found naturally in citrus fruits and coffee. This versatile, FDA-approved additive stabilizes other ingredients and enhances the product's flavor, color, and (for bars) coating.

Energy products also use other approved preservatives. Body Fuel 750, for instance, is thickened and stabilized by xanthan gum. This also appears in dairy products and salad dressings.

PowerBars include glycerine, a slightly sweet oil that helps the bar stay moist. It, too, has no known toxicity.

Additives

Most of the worst-sounding ingredients in energy products are actually good for you. Many of these are forms of vitamins or minerals that are also common in other processed foods. When you see a cereal touted as "enriched" or "fortified," for example, this means it has some of these ingredients. All are regarded as safe by the FDA.

To get vitamin E in a sports drink, manufacturers include alpha tocopherol acetate; for vitamin C, ascorbic acid; for vitamin B_{12}, cyanocobalamin is added; for vitamin A, beta-carotene; for niacin (vitamin B_3), nicotinamide or niacinamide; for vitamin B_6, pyridoxine hydrochloride.

Minerals are included through similar additives. The first word tells you the mineral name, while the second describes the compound used to carry it. Iron, a mineral that helps the blood transport oxygen, may be added to a drink through ferrous gluconate, ferrous fumarate, ferric phosphate, or any of several other iron-related compounds. Manganese comes from manganese glycerophosphate. Magnesium is included in the form of magnesium succinate, and potassium comes from potassium aspartate.

In most cases you don't need the vitamins and minerals provided in these products. As with protein, you already get plenty in a routine diet. But if your rides are especially long and intense, or if you cycle regularly in the heat, it's possible to become deficient in certain vitamins and minerals—additives keep this from happening.

Exceed Nutritional Beverage lists carrageenan on its label. This thickener is used in many chocolate and chocolate-flavored products. Some researchers question its long-term health effects. But in 1980 the FDA gave it GRAS status, although it suggested that more studies be done. In the decade since, nothing new has been reported, and carrageenan remains on the safe list.

One additive that has raised health questions is acesulfame K, or Sunette, which is found in the drink Hypo-Cell-FX. This sweetener (about 200 times sweeter than table sugar) received FDA approval in 1988. Earlier, a consumer group had sent several studies to the FDA indicating that animals fed acesulfame K developed more tumors than their counterparts. The studies also showed that diabetic rats had elevated blood cholesterol levels when they ingested it. After reviewing 15 volumes of studies, the FDA approved the additive.

Body Chemicals

Your body produces various chemicals that make exercise possible. Some energy product manufacturers reproduce these chemicals and put them in drinks and bars. This is based on the assumption that more is better—that adding them to your system will ensure that it works at maximum capacity.

Whether these chemicals help is debatable. Many nutritionists say they don't. But since they're chemically identical to what's produced by the body, they're relatively harmless.

An example is carnitine, which works to turn fat into energy. Others are inosine and coenzyme Q10, which help produce the energy molecule, ATP. There's also betaine, trimethylglycine, dimethylglycine, octacosanol, vitamin C, and vitamin E, which may help eliminate substances called antioxidants that cause tissue damage and aging. You can find all these chemicals in energy products.

You can also find substances that are included on the basis of just a few studies. For instance, sodium bicarbonate is an antacid that has shown promise as a performance enhancer in the lab. It supposedly neutralizes lactic acid buildup in the bloodstream during exercise. Compounds containing citrates and phosphates are said to do the same thing. Their effectiveness isn't proven, but these are commonly used substances in the food industry and pose no health risk.

Flavoring and Color

There are more than 2,000 flavors accepted by the FDA. About 500 of these are derived from natural sources, such as extracts or oils of plants. Since extracting these is an expensive process, most flavors are reproduced artificially.

By law, if a product uses any of the 2,000 accepted flavors, it doesn't need to list them. Instead, its label can simply read "natural flavors" or "artificial flavors." When you see these words on an energy product label, rest assured. All the flavors are FDA "accepted food additives" or are on the GRAS list.

Like flavors, specific coloring agents don't need to be listed by name on products. So in most cases, you'll only see the words "artificial colors" or "natural colors" on labels.

The only exceptions are the Yellow No. 5 and No. 6 dyes. These must be listed because they can cause allergic reactions. If you're sensitive to aspirin you may be at risk, so avoid products with these color additives. You'll find these dyes in cereals, desserts, pasta, and most over-the-counter and prescription drugs, as well as some energy products. Yellow No. 5, for example, is an ingredient in Exceed Fluid Replacement.

In some cases, specific natural color additives are listed on labels. Carotene and beet extract are two you might see. These usually don't work as well as artificial colors, but they're just as harmless. All colors used by food manufacturers are FDA "approved color additives."

Overall, a sports product's coloring agents—along with everything else in those imposing ingredient lists—pass minimum FDA standards. Does this mean you should use these products? Now that you know what's inside them, the choice is yours.

◼17 FAKE FATS

If you're serious about cycling, chances are good that you try to eat plenty of complex carbohydrate and avoid high-fat foods. But if your quest for good nutrition sometimes leaves you craving ice cream, fries, or double dollops of sour cream, you've probably become intrigued by the development of synthetic fat that promises to make such foods more healthful. Like sugar substitutes, phony fat is destined to take a prominent place in the American diet. But is it really a boon to health and fitness? Is it even safe?

Procter & Gamble stumbled upon its version, Olestra, nearly 20 years ago while trying to formulate a source of nourishment for premature infants. By chemically binding a sugar to the fatty acids in vegetable oil, the company researchers discovered a compound called sucrose polyester that has the look, taste, feel, and satiety value of real fat. But because sucrose polyester cannot be broken down by digestive enzymes, it passes through the body without contributing calories.

A Cholesterol Fighter?

By replacing much of the high-calorie fat in shortening, cooking oil, margarine, salad dressings, ice cream, baked goods, snack chips, and deep-fried foods, Olestra can make life easier for the weight conscious. And there might be health benefits for everyone. If initial studies prove correct, Olestra may be a potent cholesterol reducer that works by replacing some of the saturated fat in our diet and by picking up excess cholesterol in the intestines as it passes through. Better yet, sucrose polyester seems to lower only low-density lipoprotein (LDL) cholesterol (the "bad" type) without affecting high-density lipoprotein (HDL) cholesterol (the "good" variety).

But if Olestra seems too good to be true, it just might be. Because sucrose polyester acts like fat, it mixes with fat-soluble vitamins such as A and E and removes them from the body. While this problem can probably be solved by fortifying Olestra with vitamins, there are more serious issues. In P&G's initial safety study, the substance caused pituitary tumors, leukemia, abnormal liver changes, early mortality, and birth defects in rats. Some findings improved in a subsequent test, but the pituitary and liver problems persisted.

Because sucrose polyester is not absorbed by the body (implying that it should be safe), the Food and Drug Administration (FDA) exempted P&G from testing a second rodent species, something normally required of food additives that may be consumed in large amounts. But the Center for Science in the Public Interest (CSPI) petitioned P&G for additional testing, and the company agreed to perform a lifetime study of mice, putting off FDA approval indefinitely.

While P&G literature promotes the safety of Olestra on grounds that it is an all-natural substance made from sugar and vegetable oil, CSPI scientist Lisa Leffert points out that these substances have been chemically changed to produce "a new molecule that is totally foreign to the body." Because a chemical change can transform a harmless substance into a toxic one, questions about Olestra's safety were still being asked in 1990.

Just One Tiny Calorie . . .

The NutraSweet Company, another manufacturer familiar with the profits that can be generated by fake foods, unveiled its own fat substitute in 1988. Called Simplesse, this product is made of egg white or whey (a milk by-product) that has undergone a "microparticulation" process to turn it into tiny balls (50 billion per teaspoon) that mimic the texture of fat. Moreover, Simplesse is virtually cholesterol-free and has just 1.3 calories per gram, compared with 9 calories in a gram of real fat. Thus, it can drastically reduce the calorie and fat content of products such as margarine, dips, spreads, and creamy dressings. Simplesse-laced ice cream, for example, has about half the usual calories.

Unlike Olestra, however, Simplesse breaks down when heated, so it can't be used in baked or fried foods. Thus, its uses are limited to frozen and uncooked products.

The FDA reviewed NutraSweet's data and approved Simplesse for use in frozen desserts in 1990. However, CSPI has asked the FDA to require disclosure labels on any products containing Simplesse to warn people who are allergic to egg or milk proteins.

The CSPI and other health agencies see additional potential drawbacks to fake fat. First, they question whether it really benefits those trying to lose weight. As with soft drinks containing NutraSweet (aspartame), many people may simply add them to their diets instead of using them as a substitute for high-calorie foods. And others may think this gives them a license to consume more, as is often the case with "diet" drinks.

Another concern is that people will indulge in formerly fatty junk foods, leaving little room for complex carbohydrate that is rich in essential vitamins, minerals, and fiber, as well as the energy necessary for cycling and other activities. The CSPI has asked the FDA to require nutritional impact studies to determine how fake fat alters the diets of those who use it.

Will Olestra, Simplesse, and similar products be useful in reducing the fat and calorie content of the American diet, or will they, like artificial sweeteners, be another means for an overfed population to consume even more? We won't know until they're proven safe and have been on the market awhile.

18 THE POWER OF OAT BRAN

What are two magic words that have ensured hefty sales for any food product?

Oat bran, of course. Largely ignored until the late 1980s, it suddenly began selling like hotcakes. In fact, it can be found in hotcake mixes, as well as any number of cereals, pastas, breads, crackers, cookies, and other baked goods.

Cyclists who've seen oat bran touted as an ingredient in many of their favorite foods and such sports-oriented products as PowerBars may wonder what this substance has to offer—especially after a widely publicized study in 1990 suggested that, contrary to the hype, it has no extraordinary cholesterol-lowering abilities. Let's see what role oat bran plays in fitness, and whether it carries specific benefits for cyclists.

Bran's Benefits

Back in the 1960s, researchers noted the apparent ability of oats to reduce cholesterol, one of the major risk factors for heart disease. Eventually, interest in oat bran intensified with the health-and-fitness boom, enticing new studies and major ad campaigns. If you believe what you read on cereal boxes, a bowl of oats in the morning can cure all cholesterol problems.

The truth is somewhat less dramatic. In the most reliable study to date, researchers at Northwestern University Medical School found that the average person needed 35 grams (1.25 ounces) of oat bran per day for four to six weeks to lower cholesterol by about 3 percent. Reductions of 20 percent were achieved in a smaller study where participants consumed 100 grams (3.5 ounces) of oat bran daily for three weeks.

Oat bran brought the most dramatic results among those with high cholesterol levels. It was also most effective when combined with a diet low in saturated fat and cholesterol, and high in complex carbohydrate.

What seems to make oat bran work is the amount of soluble fiber it contains. Fiber is the indigestible portion of plant foods.

There are two basic types: soluble and insoluble. Soluble fiber absorbs water in the stomach and small intestine, forming a gel-like substance. It aids in digestion but also has other important benefits. Because it slows food absorption, the body's blood sugar level is kept stable—a boon to diabetics, hypoglycemics, and perhaps even cyclists seeking more stable energy sources. And in some as-yet-undefined way, soluble fiber interferes with the body's absorption of cholesterol, helping reduce its presence in the blood.

Insoluble fiber is beneficial, too. Found most abundantly in wheat bran, whole grains, beans, fruits, and vegetables, it sweeps through the digestive system largely intact, adding bulk and softness to the stool and aiding elimination. Diets high in insoluble fiber have been credited with lower rates of such digestive tract disorders as constipation, diverticulosis, irritable bowel syndrome, and even colon cancer.

As a bonus, both kinds of fiber (described jointly as "dietary fiber") can aid in weight control by filling you up without contributing excess calories.

The Best Sources of Soluble Fiber

Oat bran, though certainly a beneficial food, is not the only or best source of soluble fiber. While ⅓ cup of oat bran (28 grams) contains about 2.2 grams of soluble fiber, ½ cup of cooked black-eyed peas has about 4 grams. In fact, beans of every kind, peas, and lentils are excellent sources, as are carrots, corn, prunes, sweet potatoes, zucchini, broccoli, nuts, legumes, and bananas, apples, oranges, and many other fruits. Conveniently, complex carboydrate, the most efficient fuel for cycling, is a good source of both kinds of fiber.

If you wish to get some of your daily dose of soluble fiber from oats, the best sources are oatmeal and oat bran, which can be added to baked goods or sprinkled on foods. Both are also good sources of protein, vitamins, and minerals.

Watch Those Bran Labels

Just because oat bran is championed on a food label doesn't mean the product is a healthful one. For instance, you'd have to eat eight oat bran doughnuts (at a cost of 2,560 calories) to get the necessary 35 grams of bran. Similarly, 9 ounces of oat bran potato chips would meet the daily requirement but also supply 1,260 calories and 18 teaspoons of fat. Even instant oatmeal can contain large amounts of sodium and sugar.

Products such as cereal, bread, and muffins are more difficult to analyze, particularly since most list total dietary fiber instead of soluble fiber or oat bran content. Look for foods with more than 5 grams of dietary fiber or those that list oats or bran among the first four ingredients.

To discover the rationale behind oat bran in PowerBars, one of the most popular energy foods for cycling, *Bicycling* consulted the product's codeveloper, Brian Maxwell. He says oat bran was selected not for its cholesterol-lowering properties but for its ability to regulate absorption. "When you add oat bran to fructose and water," he explains, "the soluble fiber forms a gel that allows the bar to break down slowly and the body to absorb the carbohydrate over a longer period."

With oat bran, Maxwell continues, "you're really getting a high concentration of soluble fiber (the 'glue' that holds the product together), a little bit of protein, a bit of fat, and some significant carbohydrate, all of which fit into what we wanted." Oat bran also gives PowerBars their chewy texture. In all, a 65-gram PowerBar has a significant 12 grams of oat bran.

It's likely we'll also see corn and rice bran on food labels, since studies have shown they may be equally good at lowering cholesterol. Psyllium (pronounced *silly-um*) is being added to some cereals and could be another supermarket superstar. It comes from the husk of an Indian-grown seed grain and has long been used in over-the-counter bulk laxatives such as Metamucil. It has eight times as much soluble fiber as oat bran and has been proven to be an effective cholesterol reducer.

Adding Fiber to Your Diet

When adding more fiber of any kind to your diet, there are a few caveats: (1) Increase intake slowly to let your digestive system adjust; (2) drink more water; and (3) go easy on high-fiber foods the night before and the day of an important ride so as not to upset your system.

Remember, too, that because a little oat bran may be good, a lot is not necessarily better. No one encourages supplementing much beyond the level of 35 grams per day. You're better off getting your soluble fiber—and all of the other nutrients you need—from a varied diet that relies heavily on vegetables, fruits, and whole grains.

■19■ THE CHOLESTEROL FACTOR

While there are plenty of reasons to ride—fun, exhilaration, relaxation—one of the strongest motivators is the fear of becoming a statistic, one of the 1.5 million Americans who suffer heart attacks annually. High cholesterol (along with heredity, smoking, and high blood pressure) is one of the greatest risk factors for heart disease.

Cholesterol, a waxy, fatty lipid that's abundantly produced in the body (about 1,000 milligrams per day on average), is vital to life. But excess cholesterol in the blood, stemming from an improper diet or heredity, can collect along artery walls, forming plaque and leading to a condition called atherosclerosis. Even a small clot can block a narrowed artery, cutting off life-sustaining blood to the heart or brain and prompting a heart attack or stroke.

It's estimated that 25 percent of Americans have high cholesterol levels, while another 25 percent are borderline. However, just as regular exercise such as cycling can alleviate stress, reduce high blood pressure, and strengthen the heart, it can also lower cholesterol.

Cycling's Role in Lowering Cholesterol

Part of cycling's impact on cholesterol is indirect. Often, losing excess weight is all that's necessary to correct elevated blood cholesterol. Participating in an aerobic activity such as cycling is the easiest and most efficient way to lose extra pounds or maintain desirable weight.

Cycling's other effect on cholesterol is more direct. Cholesterol is carried in the blood by two types of particles: low-density lipoproteins (LDL) and high-density lipoproteins (HDL). High LDL/low HDL levels have been linked with coronary artery disease. Conversely, low LDL/high HDL levels are associated with its absence.

Know Your Cholesterol

Not surprisingly, LDL, which delivers cholesterol throughout the system, is known as "bad cholesterol"; HDL, which picks it up and returns it to the liver, is called "good cholesterol." Among the many interesting discoveries about good cholesterol is that women, who have a lower incidence of heart disease, have more of it, while heart attack victims have less.

In addition to having a low overall blood cholesterol level (under 200 mg), it's also desirable to have a high HDL-to-LDL ratio. Experts say desirable levels for HDL are more than 35 milligrams and, for LDL, less than 130 milligrams. The higher the HDL, the better. Unfortunately, raising HDL levels isn't as easy as lowering total cholesterol or LDL.

There is good news for cyclists, though. While it remains a hotly debated topic, some studies have shown that active people have higher HDL levels than sedentary people. For example, several years ago researchers at Stanford University put inactive middle-age men on a progressive walking/jogging/running program. At the end of a year, they showed HDL increases with a minimum of 8 miles a week and LDL decreases with as little as 4 miles a week. As mileage increased, so did the positive changes.

A newer Stanford study links such improvement to a loss of body fat. This time participants were divided into groups that either dieted, exercised, or did neither. Both the dieters and exercisers lost fat and experienced a 10 percent increase in HDL.

Of special interest to cyclists is that the exercisers in this study reaped other benefits as well. While they lost only fat, the dieters lost fat and muscle. Follow-ups also determined that the exercisers were more likely to keep the fat off and the HDL up. Furthermore, there's a distinct possibility that exercise without weight loss can increase HDL, and that exercise and diet together may have an even greater benefit.

Beyond weight loss and exercise, a change in diet can also dramatically lower blood cholesterol, with results often appearing in as little as three weeks. The best preventive diet is one that's low in dietary cholesterol. More important, it should be low in saturated fat, which plays an even greater role in raising blood cholesterol levels.

While it's easy to know where cholesterol lurks (only in animal foods such as meat, dairy products, and eggs), saturated fat is trickier to spot. It's abundant in animal foods but also appears in all fats and oils. Even safflower, which is the most unsaturated of oils, is 9 percent saturated. The most significant nonanimal sources of saturated fats are coconut, palm, palm kernel, and hydrogenated vegetable oils. In fact, the first few are twice as saturated as lard. Because they are so prevalent in processed foods, some experts claim that tropical oils are a more pressing issue in the battle against high cholesterol than traditional artery cloggers.

To control cholesterol, first get yours checked. Local health groups often conduct free testing at malls and hospitals. No more than 30 percent of your total calories should come from fat, and daily cholesterol intake should be below 300 milligrams (less if blood cholesterol is already at a high level), which is roughly the amount in a single egg yolk. To reduce your cholesterol even further, eat more fruit, vegetables, whole grains, monounsaturated (olive) and polyunsaturated (vegetable) oils, and fish.

Be aware that arguments persist over cholesterol and the established guidelines. There are those who contend cholesterol reduction is not beneficial for everyone, while others believe it can help us all. Fortunately, there are major new studies under way that may end the controversy.

In the meantime, there isn't anyone who'll disagree that regardless of their effect on cholesterol, cycling and a low-fat diet are two great ways to promote overall good health.

20 FIVE
NUTRITION MYTHS

Are these statements true or false? "Vitamin supplements improve performance." "Eating sugary foods before a ride causes fatigue." "Amino acid supplements make you stronger." "Vitamin

B_{15} increases the oxygen in your blood." "A high-fat diet extends endurance."

If you say true, you've been misled by some of the most common myths in sports nutrition. Such misconceptions can harm your performance—and your health. For these reasons, it's important to learn the facts behind the fallacies.

Supplements

Myth: Vitamin supplements improve performance.

Fact: They don't. Vitamins do not provide a direct source of energy. Their only purpose is to help people with vitamin and mineral deficiencies stemming from poor diets.

As a cyclist, your vitamin and mineral requirements are no greater than those of a sedentary person. And since you probably eat more than most people, it's unlikely that you're lacking any vitamin or mineral. Thus, there's no reason to pop vitamin pills.

Research shows that taking supplements does not improve the performance of well-nourished athletes. Even worse, large doses of vitamins and minerals (at least ten times the recommended dietary allowance) can be dangerous. When vitamins are consumed in quantities they function as drugs, often producing the same serious side effects. Some vitamins, for example, accumulate in the body to toxic levels. Too much niacin can cause burning or tingling of the skin, rashes, nausea, and diarrhea. It can also interfere with the body's ability to burn fat for fuel. This forces you to use glycogen at a faster rate, which makes you fatigue quicker during exercise.

If you're feeling tired or run-down, you are probably overtraining or eating too little carbohydrate for adequate glycogen synthesis. When people feel better after taking vitamin and mineral supplements, it's usually due to the strength of their belief that they'll help—the placebo effect.

Sugar and Fatigue

Myth: Eating sugary foods before a ride causes fatigue.

Fact: This old misconception used to be perpetuated even by scientists. They contended that in response to sugary foods, your body secretes insulin, a hormone that removes sugar from the blood. If you combine this effect with exercise (which also uses blood sugar), the result can be a dramatic drop in blood sugar, a condition called hypoglycemia.

While the scientists were right about this much, they were wrong about the effects of hypoglycemia. They said such low blood sugar levels would cause light-headedness, fatigue, and, in extreme cases, convulsions and even coma. This is the myth. In fact, research has since shown that low blood sugar levels have little effect on performance.

In a study at Ball State University in Indiana, cyclists were fed 300 sugar calories 45 minutes before riding to exhaustion. Though blood sugar levels decreased, performance didn't. Other studies have been even more telling, with preride sugar feedings often leading to improved efforts.

Although some people are sensitive to low blood sugar and suffer negative reactions, most can ingest sugary foods prior to riding with no adverse effects.

Amino Acids

Myth: Amino acid supplements make you stronger.

Fact: Muscle magazines are littered with the false implication that if you take amino acid supplements, your physique will soon resemble Schwarzenegger's. But the claims that amino acids increase muscle mass and decrease body fat simply aren't valid. Nor is the assertion that amino acid supplements are somehow more rapidly digested and absorbed than amino acids from food.

In fact, it's much easier (and cheaper) to get your amino acids from your regular diet. Amino acids are the chief components of protein. During the digestion of food, enzymes break down the protein, and these crucial acids are absorbed into your system. Just 1 ounce of beef, chicken, or fish supplies 7 grams of protein and 7,000 milligrams of amino acids. To equal this amount, you would need to take about 20 capsules.

The long-term risks of amino acid supplements are still unknown. But excess amino acids from whatever source do present immediate dangers. The surplus is incorporated into new protein, used for energy, or converted to fat. These processes use a great deal of water, thus increasing your risk of dehydration. In addition, large quantities of amino acids can flood your kidneys with too much protein, which then accumulates in joints, causing painful, goutlike inflammation.

Vitamin B$_{15}$

Myth: Vitamin B$_{15}$ increases the oxygen in your blood.

Fact: Not only are there many wondrous claims about this substance's imaginary powers, but the substance itself is also a myth. Vitamin B$_{15}$ is no vitamin at all. Sometimes referred to as pangamic acid or D$_{15}$, it has no chemical identity. A company can market anything it wants under the name B$_{15}$.

Researchers have found that the concoctions usually peddled as B$_{15}$ have no performance-enhancing qualities. In fact, a common B$_{15}$ ingredient has been linked to cancer. In addition, this type of unregulated "vitamin" is more likely to contain dangerous contaminants or unhealthful chemical mixes. Despite claims that B$_{15}$ increases the body's ability to use oxygen, the Food and Drug Administration has labeled the product as nothing more than a food additive. As such, it has no usefulness for cyclists.

Fat and Endurance

Myth: A high-fat diet extends endurance.

Fact: A 1983 study by Stephen Phinney, M.D., is to blame for this misconception. In the study, cyclists were able to ride just as long on a high-fat diet as they could on a diet containing 50 percent carbohydrate.

However, what works in a medically supervised lab doesn't always make sense on the road. A high-fat diet can cause disturbances in heart rhythm and is a major contributor to heart disease.

In terms of performance, such a diet limits you to submaximal efforts. In fact, it's impossible to ride above 75 percent intensity on a diet that's primarily fat. Even the cyclists in Phinney's study rode at only 63 percent of their peak ability.

A high-carbohydrate diet, on the other hand, allows you to go hard—and carries none of the health risks. Recent research has compared high-fat and high-carb diets and found that in terms of health and performance, there really is no comparison.

Part Five
RIDING TO LOSE— WEIGHT!

![21] TWO CASE HISTORIES

Case 1: Since Jerry took that 40-hour-per-week desk job one year ago, he's slowly gained weight—10 pounds to be exact. But although he's inactive during the week, he rides 100 miles on the weekends. He credits his good appetite with providing the necessary energy for such vigorous workouts. Meanwhile, the 10 pounds stubbornly remain.

Case 2: Andrea is a compulsive waistline watcher. In fact, that's the reason she rides an hour each day. She has what she considers a meager diet, but occasionally succumbs to her weakness for sweets. Nevertheless, she can't rid herself of 15 unwanted pounds. Shouldn't riding compensate for those extra scoops of ice cream?

Watch What You Eat

Contrary to popular belief, cycling doesn't give you a license to eat whatever you want, especially if you're trying to lose weight. For this, you have to do more than just strap on a helmet and ride. You must amend your eating habits.

If you want to lose weight, your goal should be to trim 500 calories per day from your diet. Since 3,500 calories constitute a pound of body fat, doing so will result in your losing 1 pound per week. And it can be done simply by eliminating unnecessary foods.

The worst culprits are fatty dressings and spreads—sour cream, butter, cream sauces, and the like. According to studies, it's easier for the body to store fat calories than carbohydrate calories. Thus, it's more likely that the former will remain in your system as excess body fat.

Replace Fats with Carbos

In addition, fatty foods are more calorically dense. For instance, 1 gram of fat contains 9 calories, while a gram of carbohydrate has just 4. One tablespoon of butter (100 percent fat) has 123 calories, whereas the same amount of fruit conserve (100 percent carbohydrate) contains 42. So the most effective way to lose weight is to substitute high-carbo foods for their high-fat counterparts.

The problem is that most dieters don't do it this way. In their quest for quick results, they make drastic cuts in food intake. This can result in nutritional deficiencies that severely compromise a cyclist's energy reservoirs and performance. Though the bathroom scale may show a dip, much of the initial loss is water, not body fat. And on such a low-energy diet, you'll probably be too tired to sustain your mileage. Thus, you'll expend fewer calories, lose less weight, and, in frustration, return to your original eating habits. In the game of weight control, you're back where you started.

The other common mistake is cutting back on energy-rich carbohydrates such as pasta, bread, rice, and potatoes. Carbohydrate is your body's most efficient kind of fuel. During a moderately intense ride, you derive energy from both carbohydrate and fat. But as your intensity increases, so does the reliance on the former. And unlike fat stores, which are almost unlimited, carbohydrate reserves can be depleted. Therefore, decreasing your intake of carbohydrate can undermine your cycling performance.

Revamp Your Diet

Now let's consider the two case studies at the start of this chapter.

Case 1: Jerry

At 5-feet-10 and 180 pounds, Jerry wants to lose 10 pounds.
Cycling: 7 hours each weekend (2,100 calories per ride at 15 mph).

Current diet: 3,100 calories (weekdays), 3,500 calories per day (weekends). Daily intake is 38 percent carbohydrate, 47 percent fat, 15 percent protein.

Breakfast: fried eggs with bacon, toast with butter and jam, coffee with half-and-half. *Snack:* doughnut, coffee with half-and-half. *Lunch:* ham and cheese sandwich with mayonnaise, potato chips, cole slaw, soda. *Snack:* chocolate bar, whole milk. *Dinner:* beef steak, mashed potatoes with gravy, beer, coffee cake. *Weekends:* extra pie or ice cream.

Problem: Diet is filled with fat (butter, pastries, bacon) and empty calories from nutrient-poor beer.

Advice: Reduce food intake by 500 calories per day. Keep diet filling by substituting carbohydrate for fat. Limit (but don't eliminate) vices such as beer.

New diet: 2,600 calories (weekdays), 3,000 calories per day (weekends)—62 percent carbohydrate, 23 percent fat, 15 percent protein.

Breakfast: pancakes with syrup and margarine, coffee with low-fat milk, orange. *Snack:* English muffin with Cheddar cheese, low-fat milk. *Lunch:* chicken breast sandwich with tomato, three-bean salad, potato, grapes, apple juice. *Snack:* chocolate bar, low-fat milk. *Dinner:* spaghetti with meatballs, Parmesan cheese, salad with low-fat dressing, melon, fig bars. *Weekends:* ice cream, cookies, beer.

Case 2: Andrea

At 5-feet-5 and 140 pounds, Andrea wants to lose 15 pounds.

Cycling: 1 hour per day at 17.5 mph (600 calories).

Current diet: 2,300 calories. Daily intake is 53 percent carbohydrate, 39 percent fat, 8 percent protein.

Breakfast: orange juice, bagel with cream cheese, coffee with half-and-half. *Lunch:* whole-milk yogurt, crackers with peanut butter, cola. *Snack:* chocolate cake, nuts, cola. *Dinner:* baked potato with sour cream, salad with French dressing, cola. *Snack:* fudge, premium ice cream.

Problem: Most of her food choices are high in fat, such as peanut butter, nuts, sour cream, and ice cream. Such a meager breakfast and lunch leave her hungry by late afternoon and evening, when she succumbs to her cravings.

Advice: Reduce food intake by 500 calories per day. Make breakfast and lunch more substantial by relying on carbohydrate and limiting fat. Eat low-fat snacks to stave off hunger. Limit treats.

New diet: 1,800 calories—62 percent carbohydrate, 20 percent fat, 18 percent protein.

Breakfast: bran cereal with low-fat milk, banana, juice, coffee with low-fat milk. *Snack:* bagel with jam. *Lunch:* turkey breast sandwich with tomato and mustard, low-fat milk, gingersnaps. *Snack:* apple, air-popped popcorn. *Dinner:* baked potato with chili, steamed broccoli, salad with low-calorie dressing, ice cream. *Snack:* fruit salad.

Eight Tips

Now that we've seen how to devise weight-loss diets for typical riders like Jerry and Andrea, let's talk about you. Here are eight tips to help you modify your eating habits in a way that will not only eliminate excess body fat but also supply the energy to ride even better.

1. Keep a food diary. Record all the foods and drinks you consume on three consecutive weekdays and one weekend day. Include oils used in cooking, cream in coffee, and dressings and sauces added to meats and vegetables, plus snacks. At the same time, record your workouts. Later, see if there's a pattern. Do you eat more high-fat snacks after a hard ride? Are your calories distributed evenly throughout the day? Are your weekend eating habits disrupting your weight-loss program?

2. Be realistic. If you try to lose more than 1 or 2 pounds a week, it'll become too difficult to diet and get the necessary nutrients for riding. A pound a week is plenty.

3. Replace the bad with the good. Decrease intake of calorically dense fat while increasing the amount of carbohydrate. Specifically, limit these high-fat items: nuts, peanut butter, salad dressings, mayonnaise, fried chicken, fatty beef, luncheon meats, butter, margarine, ice cream, whole milk, cheese, and packaged goods including most crackers, cookies, and chips containing butter, lard, or oils. If a product contains more than 4 grams of fat per 100-calorie serving, either limit your intake or pass it up.

Substitute these low-fat alternatives: whole grain cereals and breads, low-fat milk and yogurt, bagels, English muffins, turkey and chicken breast, lean meat, steamed or raw vegetables, pasta with tomato sauce, baked or boiled potatoes, squash, brown rice, bean or lentil soup, sorbet, and angel food cake. Likewise, instead of high-calorie drinks such as chocolate milk, ice-cream sodas, and beer, try water, seltzer, or juice diluted with sparkling water. And consider carrying these snacks in your jersey pocket: fresh or dried fruit, raw vegetables, fig bars, rice cakes, or bagels.

4. Don't skip meals. Three low-fat meals, plus snacks, will stave off hunger while providing essential nutrients and energy for riding.

5. Decrease high-calorie portions. Reduce the size and number of high-calorie servings. For example, eat one scoop of ice cream instead of two, four cookies instead of half the bag, or two slices of pizza instead of three.

6. Reward yourself. Don't avoid the foods you crave. You'll feel deprived and probably binge on something else. Instead, occasionally treat yourself to your favorite snack even if it's high in fat. A good time for such a treat is after your hardest ride of the week.

7. Don't starve yourself. If you overeat one day, don't fast the next to compensate. Simply accept the transgression and start anew the morning after.

8. Ride more. For weight loss, you need to disturb the equation between calories consumed and calories burned. There are two choices: You can either eat less or burn more. This discussion has dealt with the former, but the latter works just as well. Increasing your mileage while keeping your food intake constant will result in the loss of body fat.

Cycle at a speed you can maintain for at least an hour. Do this three or four times a week and you'll burn 1,400 to 2,000 calories (for a 140-pound person). Combined with other daily activities, as well as the natural calorie burning your body does just to stay alive, eventually the scales will tip in your favor.

22 EIGHT-WEEK WEIGHT-LOSS PROGRAM

In two months, you'll be 8 to 16 pounds lighter.
That's the goal of this unique weight-loss program for cyclists.

Imagine. If you start in April, by June you'll be carrying one less "spare tire" up every hill. You'll be wearing Lycra without feeling self-conscious. And in a sport where extra ounces can be a handicap, you'll be without a bowling ball's worth of fat.

But the best part is that you can reach this new level of litheness not by following some draconian diet that leaves your stomach rumbling, but by choosing your favorite foods from a varied list and (get this) doing nothing more complicated than riding your bike.

It may sound too good to be true, but the key to this program is not to be concerned about calories. As a cyclist, you must learn to judge food by its nutritional value rather than the calories it contains. Otherwise, you might not have enough energy to fuel your riding. Instead, you should focus on fat. It's much less complicated to monitor, and it's what causes you to gain weight. When you eat fatty food—a hamburger, for instance—your system is more likely to convert it to body fat. But when you eat nutritious food rich in carbohydrate, such as spaghetti, it's more likely to be used for energy.

Cut Out the Fat

Fatty foods are also a more concentrated caloric source. For example, that hamburger probably has three times the calories (and 30 times the fat) of the spaghetti. Fewer calories are burned during digestion when fatty food is involved.

Unfortunately, the average American diet is high in fat. Most of this comes from the usual list of suspects: cheese, creamy salad dressings, mayonnaise, oils, hot dogs, bacon, nuts, crackers, chips, candy bars, and cookies. Even though these fat sources are well known, they still tempt their way into our diets.

By following the recommendations of two sports nutritionists, Jeanine Barone and Andrea Boyar, your consumption of fat will be at the recommended 20 to 30 percent level. This will be a significant reduction if your diet is like that of most Americans. If you already eat well and are low in body fat, this plan will maintain your good condition.

In this program, fat portions (FPs) are the crucial measure. If a food contains 4 to 5 grams of fat, it is said to have one FP.

Likewise, 2 to 3 grams is equivalent to half an FP. If a food contains less than this, its FP is essentially zero.

To lose weight, you simply need to limit the number of FPs you consume. All men—regardless of their weight—should limit FPs to ten per day. Women, because they naturally have more body fat, should restrict their daily FPs to eight.

The Menu Planner

Devise your diet by choosing one meal per day from each of the four groups in the Menu Planner on page 92. Note the FP value of each meal, and make sure you don't exceed your daily allotment. For instance, you might choose breakfast 3, lunch 6, dinner 7, and snack 8. This menu supplies nine FPs for men and eight for women. (Women's serving sizes and FPs are listed in parentheses whenever they differ.) Unlike diets that prescribe specific and rigid meal plans for each week, this program allows you to repeat your favorite foods while ignoring your least favorites.

At the same time, ride regularly. As your mileage increases, it's natural to eat more. This is okay as long as you keep your FPs in check. In addition, your riding will enable you to occasionally enjoy high-calorie treats that would be taboo for sedentary dieters. For instance, after your longest ride each week, reward yourself with a piece of chocolate cake or some other favorite. The exercise compensates for such digressions.

Staying active also prevents your metabolism from slowing, a problem with diets that don't include exercise. With fewer calories coming in and little activity, your system slows and burns calories at a reduced rate. With such a low metabolism, it becomes easier to gain weight should you violate your diet. In addition, dieting without exercising usually leads to the loss of lean muscle tissue, which means less strength rather than less fat.

Since individual metabolisms vary, this plan may not be perfect for everyone. However, in most cases it should produce a healthy weight loss. If you reach a week when your weight seems to stabilize, don't get frustrated. Many people encounter such plateaus. Just stay with the program, keep cycling, and you'll get past it.

(continued on page 100)

The Menu Planner

Choose one menu per day from each group.

Breakfast

1. 1½ bagels (1 for
    women)
    3 tsp. margarine (2)
    1 orange
    1 cup skim milk
    FP = 3 (2 for women)

2. 1 cup skim milk
    1 bran muffin
    1 Tbsp. marmalade
    6 oz. orange juice
    FP = 2

3. 4 pancakes (2)
    ¼ cup maple syrup
    2 oranges (1)
    1 cup skim milk
    FP = 2 (1)

4. 2 slices French toast
    ⅓ cup jam
    1 banana (½)
    1 cup skim milk
    FP = 2

5. ½ grapefruit
    2 slices whole wheat
    toast (1)
    2 Tbsp. fruit conserve
    (1)
    1 tsp. margarine
    1 cup skim milk
    FP = 1

6. 1 scrambled egg
    2 slices rye toast (1)
    1 peach
    1 cup skim milk
    FP = 2

7. ½ cup oatmeal
    1 apple
    2 Tbsp. raisins
    1 cup skim milk
    FP = ½

8. ⅓ cup bran cereal
    1 cup skim milk
    ¼ cup strawberries
    1 slice whole wheat
    toast
    1 tsp. margarine
    6 oz. orange juice
    FP = 1

9. 1 cup low-fat yogurt
    ½ cup apple slices
    1 English muffin
    1 tsp. margarine
    FP = 1

10. 2 slices raisin toast (1)
    1 Tbsp. peanut butter
    6 oz. orange juice
    FP = 2

Lunch

1. 3 oz. turkey breast
   2 tsp. mustard
   2 slices rye bread
   1 tomato slice
   2 apples (1)
   2 fig bars
   FP = 2

2. 1 cup chunky beef soup
   3 oz. water-packed
     tuna
   1 tomato slice
     lettuce
   1 Tbsp. diet mayon-
     naise
   2 slices whole wheat
     bread
   1 cup fruit salad
   FP = 2

3. Taco:
     2 oz. lean ground
       beef
     1 tortilla shell
     2 tomato slices
       lettuce
     1 Tbsp. salsa
     1 peach
     1 cup skim milk
   FP = 4

4. 2 pizza slices (1)
   1 cup mixed greens
   1 Tbsp. low-calorie
     dressing
   1 apple
   FP = 4 (2)

5. 1 cup pea soup
   2 oz. lean ham
   1 oz. Swiss cheese (0)
   1 tomato slice
     lettuce
   1 tsp. mustard
   2 slices rye bread
   1 orange
   FP = 3 (2)

6. Chicken salad:
     ½ roasted chicken
       breast
     1 Tbsp. diet mayon-
       naise
     1 tomato slice
     2 slices whole
       wheat bread
     ½ cup raw carrot
       strips
     10 grapes
     1 cup skim milk
   FP = 2

(continued)

Lunch—*continued*

7. Salad:
    - 2 cups spinach, green peppers, kidney beans, mushrooms
    - 1 hard-cooked egg, chopped
    - 1 slice lean bacon, chopped
    - 2 Tbsp. low-calorie dressing
    - 1 tangerine
    - 1 cup skim milk

    FP = 3

8. 1 cup vegetable soup
    4 oz. lean roast beef (2)
    2 tsp. mustard
    1 tomato slice
    lettuce
    2 slices rye bread
    1 cup skim milk
    1 pear

    FP = 4 (3)

9. 1 cup mixed fruit
    1 cup low-fat cottage cheese
    4 whole grain crackers
    4 gingersnaps

    FP = 2

10. 1 cup chicken noodle soup
    1 baked potato
    ½ cup steamed broccoli
    1 Tbsp. melted American cheese
    1 apple

    FP = 3

Dinner

1. 2 cups pasta (1)
    ½ cup tomato/meat sauce
    1 Tbsp. Parmesan cheese
    ½ cup steamed green beans
    1 slice Italian bread
    1 tsp. margarine
    2 apricots

    FP = 3

2. 5 oz. roasted turkey breast (4)
    ¼ cup bread stuffing
    2 Tbsp. gravy, skimmed of fat
    1 cup steamed zucchini and yellow squash
    Salad:
    - ¼ cup mushrooms
    - 2 slices tomato
    - 1 cup romaine lettuce
    - 1 Tbsp. low-calorie dressing

    FP = 3

3. 2 cups pasta (1½)
   ¼ cup clam sauce
   2½ Tbsp. Parmesan
     cheese (2)
   1 roll
   ½ cup steamed green
     beans
   Salad:
     1 cup mixed greens
     2 slices tomato
     1 Tbsp. low-calorie
       dressing
FP = 2

4. 5 oz. baked flounder
     or sole with lemon
   1 baked potato
   1 tsp. margarine
   ½ cup steamed broc-
     coli
   1 cup raw spinach
     salad
   1 Tbsp. low-calorie
     dressing
   1 orange
FP = 2

5. 1 cup lentil soup
   5 oz. braised veal chop,
     lean (4)
   1 cup steamed broc-
     coli and carrots (½)
   1 roll
   1 tsp. margarine
   1 cup fruit salad
FP = 3

6. Enchilada:
     2 oz. lean ground
       beef
     ½ cup kidney beans
     1 tortilla
     ¼ cup tomato sauce
     1 Tbsp. salsa
     1 oz. Cheddar
       cheese
     ½ cup rice
     ½ cup pineapple
       chunks
FP = 4

7. 1 cup chili with meat
     and beans
   2 slices whole wheat
     bread
   1 cup mixed greens
   1 Tbsp. low-calorie
     dressing
   ½ cup mixed berries
FP = 4

8. Eggplant Parmesan:
     4 oz. broiled egg-
       plant
     1 Tbsp. Parmesan
       cheese
     ½ cup tomato sauce
   Salad:
     1 cup romaine
       lettuce
     ¼ cup raw carrots
     1 Tbsp. low-calorie
       dressing
     1 slice French bread
     1 apple
FP = 1

(continued)

The Menu Planner—*Continued*
Dinner—*continued*

9. 4 oz. lean hamburger, grilled
1 Tbsp. ketchup
1 baked potato
½ cup steamed peas and carrots
1 hamburger roll
1 peach
FP = 4

10. 2 skinless chicken legs sautéed in ½ cup tomato sauce
1 roll
½ cup steamed green beans
½ cup steamed mushrooms
1 pear
FP = 4

Snacks

1. 8 rye crackers (4)
1 oz. Swiss cheese
FP = 2

2. 2 rice cakes (1)
2 Tbsp. peanut butter (1)
2 pretzels
FP = 4 (2)

3. 6 gingersnaps (3)
½ cup berries
FP = 2 (1)

4. 4 Tbsp. raisins (2)
¼ cup mixed nuts
FP = 4

5. 1 slice angel food cake
1 cup skim milk
FP = 0

6. 1 bran muffin
1 cup skim milk
FP = 1

7. 2 cups air-popped popcorn
½ cup regular ice cream
FP = 1

8. 1 cup ice milk
1 cup banana slices (½)
FP = 1

9. 4 graham crackers
1 cup low-fat yogurt
FP = 1

10. 1 cup dry cereal
1 cup sherbet
FP = 1

TABLE 22–1.
Fat Portion (FP) Exchanges

Food	Amount Equaling 1 FP	Food	Amount Equaling 1 FP
Dairy Products and Eggs			
Cheese		Milk	
American, Edam, Cheddar	½ oz.	Skim	unlimited
		Low-fat (1%)	2 cups
		Low-fat (2%)	1 cup
Gouda, Muenster, Swiss	⅔ oz.	Whole	½ cup
		Milkshake	½ cup
Parmesan	3 Tbsp.	Nondairy creamer	3 Tbsp.
Cottage cheese		Yogurt, plain or fruit	
Low-fat (1%)	2 cups	Frozen	2 cups
Regular (4%)	½ cup	Low-fat	1 cup
Egg, whole	1	Regular	½ cup
Half-and-half	3 Tbsp.		
Ice cream	⅓ cup		
Ice milk	1 cup		
Fats/Oils			
Butter, soft or stick	1 Tbsp.	Nuts (except pistachios)	1 Tbsp. (5)
Cream cheese	1 Tbsp.	Pistachios	18–20
Margarine		Salad dressing	
Diet	1 Tbsp.	Low-calorie	2 Tbsp
Soft or stick	1 Tbsp.	Regular	2 Tbsp.
Mayonnaise		Sour cream	2 Tbsp.
Diet	1 Tbsp.	Vegetable oil	1 Tbsp.
Regular	1½ tsp.		

(continued)

TABLE 22–1—*Continued*

Food	Amount Equaling 1 FP	Food	Amount Equaling 1 FP	
Fish and Seafood				
Clams	10 oz.	Salmon	4 oz.	
Cod, flounder, scallops, sole, tuna in water	unlimited	Shrimp	16 oz.	
Meat/Poultry				
Beef		Ham		
Flank, chuck, lean	2½ oz.	Lean, cured	3 oz.	
		Regular, cured	1½ oz.	
Ground (10% fat)	1½ oz.	Leg of lamb, lean, roasted	3 oz.	
Round steak, lean	3 oz.	Pork		
Beef frankfurter	½	Bacon	1 strip	
Chicken		Canadian bacon	2 oz.	
Breast, no skin	1	Loin chop, lean	2 oz.	
Breast, with skin	¼–½	Turkey breast, no skin	8 oz.	
Drumstick	2	Veal	3 oz.	
Thigh	1			
Other Protein Foods				
Chick-peas	1 cup	Kidney beans	4 cups	

Food	Amount Equaling 1 FP	Food	Amount Equaling 1 FP
Black beans, lentils	5 cups	Lima beans, split peas	6 cups
Snacks/ Desserts			
Brownies	¾ oz.	French fries, onion rings	7
Cake	1 oz.		
Cheesecake	⅓ slice	French toast, with or without syrup	1
Chocolate	½ oz.		
Cookies		Fudge	1 oz.
Chocolate chip, sugar, cream-filled	2	Muffins	1
		Pancake, with or without syrup	1
Fig bars	5		
Corn or potato chips	1 oz.	Popcorn	
		Air-popped	
Crackers	5	Popped in oil	3 cups
Doughnut	⅓ whole	Pound cake	½ oz.
Soups			
Black bean	2½ cups	Minestrone	2½ cups
Chicken broth w/ rice and vegetables	5 cups	New England clam chowder	1½ cups
Cream of mushroom	¾ cup		

After the Program

Of course, you can't keep eating from these four groups forever. To broaden your diet, consult the FP exchanges in table 22-1 on page 97. Using this, you can substitute a variety of foods while not exceeding your recommended FPs. This lets you continue to eat healthfully without risking a midnight chip-and-dip binge.

Long after you've lost excess weight, keep in mind the concepts that helped you do it. Remember that packaged, processed foods are often high in fat. Many of these foods don't list fat content on the label. But if they do, and the product has more than 20 grams per serving, leave it on the supermarket shelf. Those 20 grams translate into four to five FPs, about half your daily limit.

Having a healthful diet doesn't mean avoiding fatty foods altogether. Enjoy them occasionally. Consider them part of the reward for being a cyclist. Then return to low-fat foods such as whole grains, fruits, vegetables, skinless poultry, and fish. This—along with regular exercise—is the basis of a sound diet.

Testimonials

Daniel Kobal, 49, of Riverdale, New York, weighed nearly 200 pounds and had elevated blood pressure and cholesterol. Then he started eating more fish, chicken, and vegetables in addition to cycling 10 miles each weekday and 50 to 60 miles on weekends. Four months later, he weighed 157 and had improved his health considerably.

"I've been far from suffering," says Kobal, a stock market analyst. "In fact, I don't even feel like I'm on a diet. I've just altered my eating habits. I even eat more than I usually would the few days before a long ride because I know my weight will stay on target."

Bernie Weisberg, 44, of Pleasanton, California, was a hefty 232 pounds. But in six months he dropped 57 pounds, mainly by becoming conscious of dietary fat and rediscovering the bike. Now he rides 200 miles a week, with occasional centuries.

"Cycling took my mind off the pounds," explains Weisberg, who manages a computer software company. "I went from watching the scale to watching the mileage. Even if I'm not dropping weight each week, the increasing mileage is an accomplishment that keeps me going. As for my diet, I now go for pasta with tomato sauce and spices or a plain baked potato with salsa. No fried foods for me."

Bud Dolfinger, 47, of Smithtown, New York, once weighed 280 pounds. He used a six-month liquid diet to get his weight to 168. But it's been cycling, plus a healthful low-fat diet of fruits, vegetables, and chicken that's helped him maintain this weight.

"When I first went on the diet, I had so much energy I felt like a caged animal," says Dolfinger, a real estate appraiser. "Cycling was a way to relieve tension and make the weight loss easier. Now I do triathlons."

23 *BICYCLING'S* CALORIE COUNTER

How many calories did you burn on today's ride? It's a simple question that, until now, was unanswerable. Granted, you could estimate your caloric consumption according to averages based on weight and speed. But the results were general and didn't account for all the factors that can affect cycling.

This chapter will change that. For the first time, you'll be able to calculate how many calories you burn on a specific ride. And by factoring in terrain, wind, riding position, and drafting, as well as speed and body weight, you'll arrive at perhaps the best estimation of caloric expenditure ever devised for cyclists. If you're counting calories, this is the formula for success.

A New Method

Calories are stores of energy contained within the three main food compounds—carbohydrate, fat, and protein. Humans break down these compounds and use a portion of the resulting energy to power the basic physiological processes of life. Thus, you burn calories just being alive. In fact, during normal daily activities, the rate is about 0.01 calorie per pound per minute. So if you weigh 150 pounds, you consume approximately 1.5 calories per minute, or 2,160 calories in 24 hours.

The remainder of the energy is either stored as excess weight or used to contract muscles for more strenuous movement and exercise. The choice is yours. Accumulate about 3,500 unused fat calories, for instance, and you'll gain 1 pound. But ride regularly and your body will burn these extra calories for energy.

During any aerobic exercise, oxygen is required for caloric combustion. Specifically, one liter of oxygen is used for every five calories burned. Thus, the way physiology labs have traditionally estimated caloric expenditure is by measuring the amount of oxygen consumed.

James Hagberg, Ph.D., and his colleagues at the University of Florida were among the first to take this technology out of the laboratory and into the real world. Using mobile equipment, they studied the caloric expenditure of cyclists on the road. Now, using their formula and a calculator, you can put this information to work for you. Of course, due to the complex nature of the variables involved, no simple formula will ever be exact. And indeed, this one is based on some estimations and generalities. The bottom line, however, is that it works, and it can give you new insight to your calorie consumption.

Your Starting Point

First, consult table 23-1 on the opposite page to determine your starting point. It's the number that appears where your weight and speed intersect. For instance, if you weigh 150 pounds and averaged 15 mph on the ride you're analyzing, then your baseline value is 8.4. Later, you'll add and subtract from this number depending on the factors that influenced your ride.

If you pedaled at a fairly constant rate throughout the ride, then average speed is suitable for computing baseline value. However, if there were parts where your speed increased or decreased significantly, then divide the ride into several portions and calculate each segment separately. For instance, on a 3-hour ride, one hour might have been spent at 20 mph, another at 18 mph, and a third at 16 mph. Although the average speed is 18 mph, you actually burned more calories than if you had maintained this rate throughout.

The reason is simple. As you go faster, air resistance and energy expenditure increase exponentially. Raising your speed 2 mph for 60 minutes gives you a calorie-burning boost that's not entirely offset by decreasing your speed 2 mph for the same period.

TABLE 23–1.
Baseline Values

Speed (mph)	Coefficient (cal/lb/min)	Calorie Expenditure (cal/min)								
		120 lb	130 lb	140 lb	150 lb	160 lb	170 lb	180 lb	190 lb	200 lb
8	0.0295	3.5	3.8	4.1	4.4	4.7	5.0	5.3	5.6	5.9
10	0.0355	4.3	4.6	5.0	5.3	5.7	6.0	6.4	6.7	7.1
12	0.0426	5.1	5.5	6.0	6.4	6.8	7.2	7.7	8.1	8.5
14	0.0512	6.1	6.7	7.2	7.7	8.2	8.7	9.2	9.7	10.2
15	0.0561	6.7	7.3	7.9	8.4	9.0	9.5	10.1	10.7	11.2
16	0.0615	7.4	8.0	8.6	9.2	9.8	10.5	11.1	11.7	12.3
17	0.0675	8.1	8.8	9.5	10.1	10.8	11.5	12.2	12.8	13.5
18	0.0740	8.9	9.6	10.4	11.1	11.8	12.6	13.3	14.1	14.8
19	0.0811	9.7	10.5	11.4	12.2	13.0	13.8	14.6	15.4	16.2
20	0.0891	10.7	11.6	12.5	13.4	14.3	15.1	16.0	16.9	17.8
21	0.0975	11.7	12.7	13.7	14.6	15.6	16.6	17.6	18.5	19.5
23	0.1173	14.1	15.1	16.4	17.6	18.8	19.9	21.1	22.3	23.5
25	0.1411	16.9	18.3	19.8	21.2	22.6	24.0	25.4	26.8	28.2

NOTE: If your weight is not listed in the table, determine your baseline value by multiplying your weight (in pounds) by the coefficient next to your speed. For instance, if you weigh 165 pounds and rode 17 mph, multiply 165 by 0.0675. The result (11.1) is your baseline value.

Once you have your baseline value, write it on line 1 of the Calorie Consumption Worksheet on the opposite page. Now it's time to adjust this number based on some key variables.

Surface Area

Air resistance is the biggest obstacle to overcome while riding. Thus, an important factor is your surface area—the size of the body you're trying to propel through the air. The ideal is to be strong and lean. This way you have lots of muscle to move minimal surface area.

One study, conducted by *Bicycling* fitness advisory board member David Swain, Ph.D., quantified the effects of size and surface area. He found that for every pound of body weight greater than 154 pounds, energy expenditure per pound decreased by approximately 0.5 percent. Conversely, caloric expenditure increased by the same amount for every pound less than 154. This means that, in most cases, larger riders can generate more power relative to their body weight and thus require less energy than smaller riders to overcome air resistance.

To apply this to yourself, calculate the difference between your weight and 154. Halve this difference and divide by 100. Then multiply the resulting number by your baseline value to derive your surface area adjustment. Write it on line 1a of the Calorie Consumption Worksheet. If you weigh more than 154, subtract this adjustment from your baseline value. If you weigh less, add it. Put the result on line 2.

Terrain

If your ride was mostly flat, put 0 on line 2a and write the same number on line 3 that you did on line 2. Then go to the next section. If your ride was hilly, read on.

Climbing at any speed burns more calories than cycling on flat ground at the same rate. Conversely, when you're descending (even if you pedal) you burn fewer calories than riding on the flats at the same rate. So the question arises, do downhills offset uphills?

For most hilly rides, the calories used while climbing and the calories saved when descending almost offset each other, but not quite. So if you rode a hilly out-and-back course, an adjustment is necessary. The reason is that as you climb, you're battling gravity. But as you descend, you don't enjoy the full advantage of

Calorie Consumption Worksheet

Line 1: Baseline Value	±	
Line 1a: Surface Area Adjustment	±	
Line 2:	±	
Line 2a: Terrain Adjustment	±	
Line 3:	=	
Line 3a: Wind Adjustment	±	
Line 4:	=	
Line 4a: Riding Position Adjustment	+	
Line 5:	=	
Line 5a: Drafting Adjustment	−	
Grand Totals:	Total Calories Burned per Minute	±	
	Total Calories Used for Life Support	−	
	Total Minutes of Riding	×	
	Total Calories Burned Riding	=	

this force. Once again, air resistance is to blame because it rises exponentially with speed, making the descent not as quick and easy as the climb is slow and hard.

Therefore, to derive an accurate measure of caloric expenditure, you need to estimate what percentage of the ride was spent climbing. Then, multiply your adjusted baseline value (line 2) by 0.01 for each 10 percent. For example, if you were climbing 30 percent of the time, multiply by 0.03. The result is your terrain adjustment. Write it on line 2a and add it to line 2. The sum goes on line 3.

Of course, not every ascent culminates in a descent. A point-to-point ride may have an overall elevation gain. If the ride you're analyzing was such, multiply your weight by the overall number of feet you climbed. The resulting number is in foot/pounds, a measure of work. For instance, if you weigh 150 pounds and took an hour to complete a course with a net elevation gain of 100 feet, you've done 15,000 (150 × 100) foot/pounds of work.

Since one foot/pound of work requires 0.0014 calories, multiply the result by this number, then divide by the total minutes ridden. Using the same example as before, the result is 0.35 calorie per minute ([15,000 × 0.0014] = 21 ÷ 60 minutes). This is the number of extra calories required per minute to climb the additional 100 feet. Put the result of your calculations on line 2a, add it to line 2, and write the sum on line 3.

If you rode a point-to-point course that has an overall decrease in elevation, follow the same steps but subtract the result from line 2.

Wind

If you rode in calm conditions, skip this section, write 0 on line 3a, and bring down the previous adjusted baseline value to line 4. If it was windy, however, you'll need to make an adjustment.

Wind, like hills, can make a ride harder or easier. With out-and-back or loop courses, the energy saved with a tailwind almost offsets the extra calories burned against a headwind. However, wind direction varies. Sometimes the headwind you battle on the ride out isn't equal to the tailwind you enjoy on the way back, or vice versa. If the wind changed in this manner during your ride, multiply the adjusted baseline value (line 3) by 0.03 (if the wind was light), 0.04 (if it was moderate), or 0.05 (if it was strong). Write the result on line 3a. If the wind was against you most of the way, add it to the adjusted baseline value on line 3. If it was with you, subtract it.

If you rode a point-to-point course with either a constant headwind or tailwind, you need to make a different adjustment. First, halve the wind speed. If it was a headwind, add this number to your actual speed. If it was a tailwind, subtract it. The result is your wind-adjusted speed. Next, refer again to table 23-1 and find the number that corresponds to the intersection of your weight and wind-adjusted speed. Subtract your original baseline value (line 1) from this number. The result is your wind adjustment, which should be entered on line 3a. Again, if you had a headwind, it should be added to line 3. If you had a tailwind, it should be subtracted. Tally the result on line 4.

For example, if you weigh 150 pounds and rode 15 mph into a 10-mph headwind, your wind-adjusted speed is 20 mph (10 ÷ 2 + 15) and your wind adjustment is 5 (13.4 [adjusted baseline value] − 8 [original baseline value]). Since it was a headwind, the result is added to line 3. Conversely, if you weigh 150 pounds and rode 15 mph with a 10-mph tailwind, your wind adjustment is 3.1 (8.4 − 5.3), which is subtracted from line 3.

Wind conditions are rarely this distinct, however. A crosswind is more common than a direct headwind or tailwind. The energy requirement of riding with most crosswinds is about 70 percent that of cycling into a headwind. Thus, to figure your wind adjustment in a crosswind, use the method described earlier, just as if you had ridden into a headwind. Then multiply the wind adjustment by 0.7 and add the result to the adjusted baseline value.

For example, if you weigh 150 pounds and are riding 15 mph in a 10-mph crosswind, your wind adjustment is 3.5 (5 × 0.7). Add this to line 3.

Riding Position

At speeds below 15 mph, there's little difference between the caloric cost of riding in an upright position and on the drops. However, when you're moving faster, riding in a crouched position burns significantly fewer calories than cycling in an upright one. Similarly, you expend less energy when your bike is free of panniers, which makes you less aerodynamic.

If you rode primarily on the drops, you don't need to adjust your baseline value. Simply enter the same number on line 5 that you did on line 4. However, if you sat upright with your hands on top of the bar or brake lever hoods, or if your bike was outfitted with panniers, consult table 23-2. Find your speed and the increase in caloric expenditure listed beside it. Multiply your adjusted baseline value (line 4) by this number, then enter the result on line 4a. Add this to line 4 and write the sum on line 5.

Drafting

Dr. Hagberg's research shows that drafting reduces workload by about 1 percent for each mph.

If you didn't draft, or if you rode alone, no adjustment is necessary on your worksheet. Conversely, if you sucked someone's wheel the entire ride, you need to turn your speed into a percentage and subtract it from the adjusted baseline value (line 5). For instance, if you rode at 15 mph, take 15 percent of your adjusted baseline value. Write the result on line 5a and subtract it from line 5.

It's more likely, however, that you drafted for only part of the ride. If this is the case, convert your speed from mph to percent as before. Then estimate what fraction of the ride you drafted and, in turn, take that percentage of your adjusted baseline value. For example, if you drafted for a third of a 15-mph ride, take 5 percent (⅓ of 15) of line 5. Enter the result on line 5a, then subtract it from line 5. This gives you the total number of calories burned per minute of riding.

TABLE 23–2.
Riding Position Adjustment

Speed (mph)	Increases in Calorie Expenditure
15	03
16	08
17	12
18	18
19	22
20	26
22.5	38
25	50

Final Adjustment

Since this result includes your body's basic physiological requirements for existence, to determine how many calories were used just for riding you need to make one final adjustment.

Multiply your weight in pounds by 0.01, which is the number of calories per pound that you burn naturally. Subtract the result from total calories burned per minute. Then multiply by the total minutes of riding. The result is the total calories burned while riding. Then think of all the calories you used just figuring this out.

24 DEFLATING YOUR "SPARE TIRE"

Spare tire. Paunch. Love handles. Michelin man middle. Whatever you call it, that ring around the waist is apparent on male cyclists of every ilk—from fun-and-fitness riders to world-class athletes. You may be fit, fast, and food conscious but still carry a spare. So where does this extra baggage come from—and how can you send it packing?

There are a few inevitabilities about fat that involve age and sex. Around age 25, the body's metabolism begins to slow and the average person tends to lose muscle and gain fat. As they age, women typically deposit fat on the thighs, buttocks, upper back, and backs of the arms. Men accumulate their fat around the waist and above the navel (the classic beer belly), making them more susceptible to heart disease. "Men are genetically predisposed to deposit fat in the abdomen first," says Randy Ice, a physical therapist who operates the SCOR Human Performance Center in Whittier, California, where many elite riders train. "It's something that happens to the best and the worst of us, from the Race Across America rider to the totally inactive slob. Even Pete Penseyres will pinch his abdomen and say, 'I'm really fat now.' His pinch is awfully dinky but, yeah, it's more than when he's in RAAM-winning shape."

For ultrafit cyclists, Ice says a bit of fat around the middle is immaterial; what really counts is total body fat. "When Penseyres complains about his roll, I'll measure his body fat and it may be 7.5 percent instead of the 6.9 percent when he's in peak shape," says Ice. "That's inconsequential. Even if you've got a roll, if you're under 10 percent total body fat [for a competitive male cyclist] that's not going to slow you. Performance and health relate to total body fat, not just what's around your middle."

While elite male runners average about 7 percent body fat and cross-country skiers 8 percent, world-class cyclists are around 9 percent. Karen Roy, a coach and former nationally ranked sprinter, says cyclists may be "fatter" than other athletes because they can afford to be. Cycling is less selective than running in terms of body type, so larger individuals can ride successfully and comfortably. Unless they're climbing, cyclists don't have to lift their weight, nor does their excess fat bounce uncomfortably as on runners.

Why Cyclists Are Prone to the Thick Middle

Roy and Ice concur that to some extent form dictates function. Cyclists aren't necessarily fatter because they ride, but may have adopted this more forgiving sport because they were heavier to begin with.

Roy also notes that a bit of extra fat on a fit cyclist isn't always a drawback. "While extra weight can be a burden, you must have a reserve for endurance," she explains. "Fit people can burn fat better. It's a readily available energy source—if you're fit enough to use it."

The tendency of male cyclists to grow around the middle also has to do with the slightly less efficient nature of the exercise. Sports such as running, cross-country skiing, and swimming work more muscle groups than cycling and can burn more calories. Moreover, cycling does nothing to strengthen the abdominal muscles. Because a strong stomach isn't crucial to the sport, most cyclists don't work at toning and tightening it, giving them a flabbier look.

But even world-class riders who work the abdominal area often appear paunchy during competition. The culprit is the cycling position. When you lean over, says Ice, the downward pull of gravity on the abdominal content makes you appear thicker in the middle.

Efficient breathing is also part of it. If you keep your stomach muscles tight while tucked, says Roy, "the organs within the abdomen press against the diaphragm, restricting its movement and making deep, heavy breathing more difficult." Top riders have learned to relax the abdomen while riding, contributing to its softer, slouchier look. The result is more efficient breathing but less flattering race photos. Says Roy of husband, coaching partner, and racer Thurlow Rogers, "He has a 32-inch waist, but I've seen pictures that make him look like he has a giant, expanding tube around his middle."

Get Rid of the Middle

While a spare tire may be a good sign for the pros, for most male cyclists it's the result of too much body fat and too little muscle tone. Here are some tips for deflating yours.

1. Have your body fat measured. Underwater weighing is most efficient, but electrical impedance and skinfold calipers are also reliable. Gyms, YMCAs, performance labs, and sports medicine specialists offer these services. For good health, a male's body fat content should be less than 15 percent. For optimum performance, it should be less than 10 percent.

2. Losing body fat requires aerobic exercise. It's good that you're cycling, but you may need to increase the length or change the intensity of your rides to lose more fat. Determine your training heart rate (for the average person, roughly 75 to 85 percent of maximum heart rate, which can be estimated by subtracting your age from 220) and maintain it. Working at too low or too high an intensity won't burn fat as efficiently.

3. Cross-train in other sports to work additional muscle groups.

4. If you aren't losing fat by exercising, examine your diet. Cutting calories may be necessary. An easy way to do so—and improve overall health and performance—is to restrict your fat intake and increase your consumption of complex carbohydrate by eating more vegetables, legumes, and whole grains for example.

5. While you can't "spot reduce" (remove fat from the abdomen only), you can increase muscle strength and firmness in that area with certain activities. These include workouts on weight-training machines such as Nautilus and Universal, rowing, aerobics, cross-country skiing, and calisthenics (sit-ups, crunches, trunk twists) with or without weights. It's important to work the entire abdominal area—upper, lower, and sides—by using a variety of exercises. A strong, flat abdomen not only improves your appearance but also protects your lower back from injury.

■25 POSTRIDE PIG-OUTS

Admit it. There have been times when you've gotten off the bike and consumed anything you could get your hands on. A bag of cookies. Multiple scoops of ice cream (Greg LeMond's favorite). A handful of candy bars. Aisle 3 at 7-Eleven.

Though not uncommon, postride binges can be unsettling, since you're probably careful about what you eat otherwise. So what causes these feeding frenzies and, more important, how can you control them? For answers, *Bicycling* went to Nancy Clark, one of America's foremost sports nutritionists.

Q. What causes postride binges?

A. Generally, when you start overeating it's because you're physiologically starving. When you get hungry your body craves quick energy, which generally is sweets. And when you're real hungry and tired, and feeling you deserve to eat because you've just ridden for 2 hours, it's easy to overdo it.

Q. Why do some riders get so hungry?

A. For a lot of people, a big motivation to exercise is losing weight. If you're riding hard—say 20 mph—you might be burning 11 calories a minute. If you're out for 60 minutes, that's 660 calories, a lot of food. If all you've had beforehand is a 200-calorie breakfast, you won't have much control when you spot an ice-cream store afterward.

Q. Can these binges be prevented?

A. Yes. Simply have a bigger breakfast. That way, you'll have the presence of mind to eat appropriately afterward.

Q. What constitutes a big breakfast?

A. In studies, subjects who ate 400 to 1,200 calories of carbohydrate 1 to 4 hours before exercising were able to prolong their endurance. What, when, and how much you eat depends on what works for you. I stress high-carbohydrate, low-fat foods and give these general guidelines for when and how much to eat: 3 to 4 hours before (700 to 800 calories); 2 to 3 hours before (200 to 400 calories); 1 to 2 hours before (blended or liquid meal, 400 calories); less than 1 hour before (100 to 200 calories).

Q. What if you ride in the late afternoon or evening?

A. Make sure you have a good breakfast and lunch. A preride snack may also be in order.

Q. Are novice riders more susceptible to postride bingeing?

A. Probably, because they don't know how to eat appropriately beforehand. I can remember going for a 60-mile ride with people who had nothing but a poached egg for breakfast. They were holding off for their big Sunday dinner when they really needed that food ahead of time.

Q. Some veteran riders claim their metabolism has adapted to cycling, and they can conserve food better on the bike. Is this possible?

A. Yes, and I think it happens when the body doesn't have fat to lose. As they get down toward their setpoint [optimum body fat percentage], they begin to get a little more energy efficient.

Q. Can eating on the bike help stave off that ravenous hunger?

A. Yes. If you're cycling for more than 90 minutes, it's important to eat something during the ride. Some cyclists use sports drinks. Some drink water and eat bananas, PowerBars, or whatever else appeals to them. What you're looking for is fluid and carbohydrate. With a sports drink, you get both in one bottle.

Q. Why do some cyclists crave particular foods after a ride?

A. Usually when you need quick energy, you crave sweets. If you're in a real calorie deficit, you may also crave fat. Common cravings like ice cream and cookies are really just a combination of the two. Sometimes when you eat too much carbohydrate before an event you crave protein afterward. A craving for salty foods means that's what your body needs. And if you crave or chew ice, that's often a sign of iron deficiency.

Q. Some cyclists aren't hungry immediately after riding but become ravenous a few hours later. Why?

A. You get really hot during exercise, and when your body temperature is elevated, it can kill your appetite. When your body temperature gets down to a more normal level, your appetite returns. When swimmers come out of the water, they tend to be ravenous because they're cold.

Q. Is there some way, during that gap when you aren't hungry, to fend off a binge?

A. A good way is to drink cold juices, which supply the carbohydrate you need in a refreshing liquid form.

Q. Earlier you implied that overeating may be partly psychological—the feeling that, "I earned this."

A. That's true. I tend to fall into that kind of thing, and I think most people do. One of the fun treats of exercising is being able to eat more. But for overall diet, cyclists need to pay as much attention to their health as people who don't exercise. You can't just say, "I ride a bike so I can eat whatever I want."

Q. Are there some guidelines for what to eat when the post-ride hungries hit?

A. The hunger is real, and you need to give your body what it wants in terms of recovery food, and that's carbohydrate. For casual riders, it's not that big a factor because they don't deplete their glycogen stores. But the harder you exercise, the more important your recovery diet becomes. I recommend 0.5 gram of carbohydrate per pound of body weight within two hours after a workout, and then the same amount again two hours later. If you weigh 150 pounds, that's 75 grams of carbohydrate or 300 calories, an amount you can get from a cup of orange juice and a bagel, or a bowl of cereal with a banana.

Q. Can a bit of frivolous eating after a ride hurt?

A. If you're eating more than 1,800 calories a day and 10 percent of these are sugar, it's still within reason. A 180-calorie treat isn't going to cause you to die of nutritional deficiencies. There's something to be said for reward foods—we're all human. Just make sure that in general you have a good, wholesome diet.

26 AVOIDING WINTER WEIGHT GAIN

As you may have already discovered, there's probably no more degenerative time for a cyclist than winter. Throughout the country, fewer hours of daylight leave less time for riding. And in certain areas, ice and snow make cycling impossible. As a result, many riders begin to balloon with unwanted pounds.

Why Do You Gain Weight?

To keep from gaining weight in winter, you first have to understand why it usually occurs. The chief reason is age. As you grow older, you gain weight easier. On the average, 60 percent of all calories ingested are used to keep your body breathing and your organs working. But as age slows these basic functions, your body requires fewer calories to maintain them. So, the result is unused calories and extra weight—even if you remain as active.

"The majority of energy expended is not in activity, but in your basal metabolic rate—just keeping your body alive," explains nutritionist Phillip Harvey, Ph.D. "Between age 20 and 25, your basal metabolic rate begins to decline by about 2 percent a year. By the time you're in your thirties and forties, your metabolism is much slower than it had been, and it's using significantly fewer calories."

Adds Art Hecker, Ph.D., another nutritionist: "If you continue to consume your usual amount of calories once your metabolism slows, the excess will be deposited as fat. So unless you work harder or reduce your calorie intake, you will gain weight."

Ironically, becoming fitter also reduces your caloric needs and increases your chance of weight gain. According to Dr. Harvey, "Training slows your metabolic rate in the same way it reduces your heart rate. When you become fit, you become more efficient at utilizing calories—so you require less."

How to Keep It Off

Each winter, as your age and fitness increase, you're more likely to gain weight. But this doesn't mean you're destined for king- or queen-size togs. In fact, there are seven ways to stay slim. Heed each one next winter and you'll feel regenerated, both physically and mentally.

1. Eat less more often. Getting most of your daily calories from a single meal overloads your system and causes rapid weight gain.

"If you consume all your calories in one or two meals instead of, say, five or more, there's an increase in the amount of fat deposited," explains Dr. Hecker. "It's called the meal-feed syndrome, and many active people do it. They'll eat no breakfast, a light lunch, and then overeat at the end of the day. The body can deal with this intake only to a certain limit, and then excess calories are diverted into fat stores."

2. Monitor your weight. If your weight increases each winter and decreases every spring, the extra poundage will gradually become easier to regain and harder to shed.

"There's a risk to saying, 'Well, okay, I might gain some weight this winter, but I'm going to lose it come spring,'" says Dr. Hecker. "When you have cyclic weight fluctuations, your body retains fat more effectively in anticipation of the expected weight loss. The best way to keep your weight steady is through daily monitoring. Then, when you notice it starting to increase, you can cut back accordingly."

3. Avoid "heavy" foods. These include sauces, dressings, and all fats—fare that's, unfortunately, most popular during the winter holidays.

"The type of food people eat in winter is much different than what they eat in summer," says Ann Grandjean, chief nutrition consultant for the U.S. Olympic Committee. "For instance, in winter, there's not as much fresh fruit available, and you're not eating as many salads."

A diet that's high in fat literally weighs you down. For instance, eat 100 calories of carbohydrate (a baked potato), and 23 calories are used to process the carbs while the other 77 go into storage. But eat 100 calories of fat (a tablespoon of butter on that baked potato) and only three calories are used in combustion while the remaining 97 become fat. For every 3,500 calories unburned, you gain about one pound.

4. Drink less alcohol. As the nights grow longer, drinking often replaces other recreational activities. Unfortunately, alcohol is second to fat as a calorie source.

"One thing it tends to do is make you hungrier," says Dr. Hecker. "You have a few drinks and then you overeat. But, more important, alcohol is an empty calorie source. There are no other nutrients coming in with it, unless you're drinking a gin and tonic and eating the lime."

5. Keep riding. Less saddle time is the most obvious reason for winter weight gain. If the roads are too slick for conventional training, try powering a mountain bike through the snow. If you dress correctly, you'll find it fun and invigorating. Plus, you'll burn more calories. "Not only is the body expending energy for exercise," explains Dr. Harvey, "but it's expending energy just to keep warm."

If the weather is extremely uncooperative, try using an indoor resistance trainer. With such a device, you can re-create an outdoor workout in your living room.

6. Try other sports. According to Grandjean, an ideal alternative for cyclists is swimming. "You'll burn four times as many calories swimming a mile as you will running a mile," she says. "Plus, there's minimal risk of injury."

Cross-country skiing is another winter calorie combustor, and it taxes many of the same muscles as cycling. Weight training is also worth considering. By spending three or four hours a week in the gym, you'll not only gain power and strength but also keep your fat levels in check.

7. Don't eat as much. It's as simple as that. If winter means you're exercising less, then you should also be eating less. Continue to follow your high-carb training season diet, but reduce the quantity.

"You can't get away with consuming 4,000 calories a day when your needs have dropped to 2,500 or 3,000," says Dr. Hecker. "If you want to avoid falling into the winter weight gain trap, eat less, or do more."

▪27▪ APPETITE CONTROL FOR GUILT-FREE HOLIDAYS

Department store lines, the suicide rate, and your waistline. These things increase during the holiday season. Unfortunately, there's not much you can do about the first two. But the third is totally within your control.

The battle isn't easy, though. As the holidays approach, several factors conspire to cause weight gain. Less daylight and bad weather keep you from riding as much, and the social climate changes as well. There are office parties, family gatherings, bowl games, and New Year's Eve—each of which commonly features large amounts of fattening food and alcohol. By the time normalcy returns in January, the damage is done and you may be lugging around several extra pounds.

Enjoy the Holidays without Extra Pounds

Fortunately, there is a way to enjoy all the holiday revelry (or any festive time such as vacation) without gaining weight. It just takes planning and willpower.

For instance, to avoid overloading on empty calories, make your first party drink a nonalcoholic beverage such as mineral water or diet soda. By starting your evening this way, you'll fill up and won't feel like drinking as much later. The advantages are twofold. You'll avoid empty alcohol calories, and your appetite won't intensify as it does when you drink too much. (The latter is largely a psychological effect that stems from fewer inhibitions and less willpower.)

The foods that dominate holiday snacking—cookies, cake, candy, pie, ice cream—are the most likely to trigger overeating, according to research. Eating sweets increases your blood sugar, which causes your pancreas to produce insulin to bring it back to normal. But insulin also stimulates the appetite. It's a vicious cycle in which you're the loser.

The best way to combat this is still the oldest way—use

willpower. But you don't have to abstain from sweets altogether. Instead, limit yourself or refrain from eating fatty treats until you've had a nutritious meal. This way, you won't be as hungry for the snacks.

It's also a good idea to keep sweets out of view. The sight and smell of such foods provide a strong stimulus to eat. Of course, sometimes the refrigerator or cupboard isn't a good enough hiding place. During those times when you're having serious problems with your willpower, you may want to get into the holiday spirit and give away the tempting treats.

Holiday Feasts

Besides endless snacks, the holidays are also characterized by huge, fat-laden feasts. From Thanksgiving until New Year's, you probably eat more meat, cheese, sauces, and gravies than at any other time of year. All these foods are high in fat. This means they're a concentrated source of calories, many of which are likely to be converted into body fat.

To lower your holiday fat intake, plan for your big meal in the same manner as you would a big ride. This means setting goals and standards for yourself and making sure you reach them.

For instance, make a point of going easy on sauces, creams, dressings, butter, and gravies. These are all-pervasive sources of fat calories. Diet products such as light margarine or light salad dressing are an excellent alternative, providing less fat and fewer calories.

It also can help to schedule your big meal for early in the day. Too many holiday feasts take place at night. When you go to sleep soon after eating, there's no immediate need for the calories you consumed. Thus, they're more likely to be stored as body fat. In addition, some people starve themselves all day in anticipation of the big meal. The result isn't pretty: an overindulged, stuffed guest with the holiday blues. It's better to eat a low-fat breakfast and lunch even on the days of big holiday meals. You'll still enjoy the feast, but you won't overindulge.

In any case, try to serve yourself medium helpings and just say no to seconds. Supplement these good habits with daily workouts on an indoor trainer or some other activity. Then maybe, for once, losing a few extra pounds won't need to be a New Year's resolution.

 CREDITS

The information in this book was drawn from these articles in *Bicycling* Magazine.

"Lessons for a New Rider" Nelson Pena, "Meals on Wheels: The True Meaning of Fast Food," May 1987.

"Eating, Drinking, and Cycling" Nelson Pena, "The Facts about Cycling Nutrition," January/February 1989.

"Fuel for Spring Training" Ellen Coleman, M.S., R.D., "The Right Stuff: Feed Your Spring Fever with Carbohydrates," March 1989.

"Building Your Endurance and Beating the Bonk" Steve Johnson, Ph.D., "Bonk: It Feels Just Like It Sounds," September 1989.

"The Good Stuff: Carbohydrate" Nelson Pena, "What Does This Man Know That You Don't?" July 1988.

"The Ideal Cycling Diet" Ellen Coleman, M.S., R.D., "The Ideal Cycling Diet: Eating for Health and Performance," April 1989.

"Liquid Energy" Ellen Coleman, M.S., R.D., "Revival of the Fittest: To Stay Fresh on Long Rides, Take a Sip of Liquid Energy," June 1989.

"Filling Your 'Inner Tube'" Nelson Pena, "Filling Your Inner Tube," April 1988.

"Five 'Recipes' for Special Occasions" Elizabeth Applegate, Ph.D., "Different Rides, Different Diets: Five 'Recipes' for Improved Performance," July 1988.

"Avoiding an Upset Stomach" Virginia DeMoss, "Queasy Rider: Coping with Exercise-Induced Nausea," July 1990.

"Buyer's Guide to Sports Drinks and Foods" Liz Smutko, "Fuel for Flying: A Buyer's Guide to Energy Drinks and Foods," July 1990.

"Alternatives to Pasta" Ellen Coleman, M.S., R.D., "Beyond Pasta: If You're Sick of Spaghetti, Try These Alternative Endurance Fuels," July 1989.

"Junk Food, Fast Food" Ellen Coleman, M.S., R.D., "Twinkie Power: How to Eat Nutritiously at Convenience Stores and Fast-Food Restaurants," August 1989.

"Make Energy-Packed Meals with Your Microwave" Virginia DeMoss, "Microwave Meals: A Cold, Hard Look at Frozen Dinners," January/February 1990.

"The News on Booze" Ellen Coleman, M.S., R.D., "The News on Booze: Alcohol's Unsettling Effect on Cycling Performance," October/November 1989.

"Are Sports Drinks and Foods Healthful?" Karen Roy, "What's in There? The Ingredients in Sports Drinks and Energy Bars Boost Performance, but Are They Healthful?" May 1990.

"Fake Fats" Virginia DeMoss, "Ersatz Fat: Do New Synthetic Foodstuffs Mean Worry-Free Indulgence?" June 1990.

"The Power of Oat Bran" Virginia DeMoss, "Magic Bran: Does an Oat-Rich Diet Benefit Cyclists?" April 1990.

"The Cholesterol Factor" Virginia DeMoss, "Cycle Away Cholesterol: Ride Your Bike to Avoid Congested Arteries," March 1990.

"Five Nutrition Myths" Ellen Coleman, M.S., R.D., "Five Nutrition Myths: The Facts behind the Fallacies," September 1989.

"Two Case Histories" Jeanine Barone, M.S., "Riding to Lose (Weight, That Is)," May 1989.

"Eight-Week Weight-Loss Program" Jeanine Barone, M.S., and Andrea P. Boyar, Ph.D., R.D., *"Bicycling's* 8-Week Weight-Loss Program: Try It. You Have Nothing to Lose but 8 to 16 Pounds," April 1990.

"*Bicycling's* Calorie Counter," James Hagberg, Ph.D., with Nelson Pena, *"Bicycling's* Exclusive Calorie Counter: Finally, a Way to Accurately Determine How Many Calories You Burn While Riding," May 1989.

"Deflating Your 'Spare Tire'" Virginia DeMoss, "Lose Your Spare Tire: Let the Air Out with Some Fat-Fighting Advice," May 1990.

"Postride Pig-Outs" Virginia DeMoss, "Post-Ride Pig-outs: How to Keep from Going Hog Wild," August 1990.

"Avoiding Winter Weight Gain" Joe Kita and Nelson Pena, "Eat, Drink, but Be Wary: Seven Ways to Avoid Winter Weight Gain," December 1987.

"Appetite Control for Guilt-Free Holidays" Ellen Coleman, M.S., R.D., "Gobble, Gobble: Tips for Avoiding a Wide Christmas," December 1989.

Photographs

Donna H. Chiarelli/Rodale Stock Images: photo 5-1; Angelo Caggiano/Rodale Stock Images: photo 8-1.